This book provides a vital, in-depth exploration of AI integration in legal education, addressing ethical, practical and sustainability challenges with remarkable insight. By critically analysing AI's role without overlooking the essential human element, it fills a crucial gap in the AI debate, offering essential guidance for both legal educators and practitioners.
Professor Michael Reynolds, *The London School of Economics*

AI and Legal Education

This book provides a comprehensive interdisciplinary analysis of the sustainable and ethical integration of artificial intelligence (AI) within legal education, offering practical strategies for balancing innovation with ethical responsibility. Discussing the intersection of legal studies, technology and ethics, the book focuses on AI's role in reshaping professional education.

With the rising demand for digital transformation in legal education and the increasing scrutiny of AI's ethical impact, this book explores the potential of AI to enhance legal learning and practice, while critically examining the challenges of data privacy, algorithmic bias and equitable access to technology. Outlining a framework for incorporating AI into the law curriculum, the book equips the readers with both cutting-edge technological skills and a deep understanding of AI's ethical and societal implications. Drawing on a wide range of sources, including industry data and academic research, the book offers grounded, actionable guidance on implementing AI in a way that promotes inclusivity, sustainability and long-term relevance. It addresses the needs of legal education institutions, faculty and students, providing them with the tools to navigate the evolving legal landscape while maintaining ethical standards.

The book will also be of interest to researchers in the fields of law, education and AI ethics.

Anil Balan is a senior lecturer in professional legal education at the Dickson Poon School of Law, King's College London, and a senior fellow of the Higher Education Academy. The research in this book relates to Anil's wider research interests on enhancement of teaching, assessment and feedback for law students from culturally diverse backgrounds, in respect of which he has published numerous peer-reviewed articles in prominent journals.

Routledge Research in the Law of Emerging Technologies

Regulating the Metaverse
A Critical Assessment
Ignas Kalpokas and Julija Kalpokienė

The Regulation of Digital Technologies in the EU
Act-ification, GDPR Mimesis and EU Law Brutality at Play
Vagelis Papakonstantinou and Paul de Hert

Privacy, Data Protection and Data-driven Technologies
Edited by Martin Ebers and Karin Sein

Social Media, Criminal Law and Legality
Laura Higson-Bliss

Web3 Governance
Law and Policy
Edited by Joseph Lee and Jyh-An Lee

AI and Legal Education
Ethical and Sustainable Approaches
Anil Balan

For more information about this series, please visit: www.routledge.com/Routledge-Research-in-the-Law-of-Emerging-Technologies/book-series/LAWTECHNOLOGY

AI and Legal Education
Ethical and Sustainable Approaches

Anil Balan

LONDON AND NEW YORK

First published 2025
by Routledge
4 Park Square, Milton Park, Abingdon, Oxon OX14 4RN

and by Routledge
605 Third Avenue, New York, NY 10158

Routledge is an imprint of the Taylor & Francis Group, an informa business

© 2025 Anil Balan

The right of Anil Balan to be identified as author of this work has been asserted in accordance with sections 77 and 78 of the Copyright, Designs and Patents Act 1988.

All rights reserved. No part of this book may be reprinted or reproduced or utilised in any form or by any electronic, mechanical, or other means, now known or hereafter invented, including photocopying and recording, or in any information storage or retrieval system, without permission in writing from the publishers.

Trademark notice: Product or corporate names may be trademarks or registered trademarks, and are used only for identification and explanation without intent to infringe.

British Library Cataloguing-in-Publication Data
A catalogue record for this book is available from the British Library

ISBN: 978-1-032-99427-7 (hbk)
ISBN: 978-1-003-86355-7 (pbk)
ISBN: 978-1-003-60739-7 (ebk)

DOI: 10.4324/9781003607397

Typeset in Times New Roman
by Apex CoVantage, LLC

Contents

	Introduction	1
1	Ethical Considerations in AI Adoption	18
2	Bias Mitigation and Fairness	34
3	Digital Divide Mitigation	50
4	Faculty Training and Development	64
5	Regulatory Compliance in AI Adoption	79
6	Data Privacy and Security	93
7	Long-Term Viability of AI Solutions	108
	Conclusion	123

Introduction

Balancing Progress and Responsibility

Artificial intelligence (AI) has emerged as a transformative force in nearly every facet of modern society,[1] and the field of legal education is no exception. In recent years, the integration of AI technologies into legal education has promised to revolutionise the way law is taught, practiced and understood. AI-driven legal tools offer the potential to streamline research, enhance access to legal resources and provide novel solutions to complex legal challenges. However, this promising revolution is not without its own set of ethical and sustainability challenges, intricately linked to the adoption and impact of AI in legal education. While AI offers unprecedented opportunities for efficiency and innovation, it also poses ethical dilemmas that demand rigorous investigation. This book explores the multi-faceted sustainability challenges that arise from the adoption of AI in legal education. Sustainability, in this context, goes beyond environmental considerations to also encompass equity, ethics and the long-term viability of AI-driven educational practices.

As noted by Oermann and Weinert, sustainability always implies ethical standards, particularly in terms of fostering a protective relationship toward both the environment and humanity across generations.[2] Becker underlines the complexity of sustainability ethics, moving beyond the notion that sustainability is just about protecting the environment or reducing resource consumption.[3] Rather, it is about considering the long-term ethical implications of actions and policies on future generations and how these actions intersect with various domains, including technology, education and law. This idea is particularly important in the context of AI adoption, where decisions made today

---

1 J. Lobera, C. J. Fernández-Rodríguez and C. Torres-Albero, 'Privacy, Values and Machines: Predicting Opposition to Artificial Intelligence' (2020) 71 *Communication Studies* 448.
2 N. O. Oermann and A. Weinert, 'Sustainability Ethics' in H. Heinrichs, P. Martens, G. Michelsen and A. Wiek (eds), *Sustainability Science* (Springer, Dordrecht 2016) 175–192.
3 C. Becker, 'Sustainability and Ethics' in C Becker (ed), *Sustainability Ethics and Sustainability Research* (Springer, Dordrecht 2012) 6–34.

DOI: 10.4324/9781003607397-1

will have far-reaching consequences for future legal professionals, students and the broader public. For instance, decisions about how data is collected, stored and used in AI systems have long-term ramifications for individual privacy and equity, especially as AI systems become more prevalent in legal education and practice. Biedenweg and colleagues also emphasise the need for sustainability ethics to be embedded in institutional decision-making processes, particularly in higher education, where ethical considerations shape curriculum development, resource allocation and the integration of new technologies like AI.[4]

The ethical implications of AI adoption cannot be understated. AI algorithms are not immune to biases, and their utilisation in legal education may perpetuate existing inequities. This book explores strategies to promote fairness, inclusivity and ethical AI practices in the legal education context, emphasising the sustainability of equity. Resource allocation strategies are examined to guide institutions in optimising investments in AI while aligning with sustainability objectives. Equally essential is the development of sustainable faculty training programmes, ensuring that educators are equipped to harness AI's potential effectively. This book navigates the intricate terrain where AI adoption and sustainability intersect in legal education. By examining these sustainability challenges and proposing strategies for their resolution, this study seeks to provide educators, policymakers and stakeholders with a comprehensive understanding of the complex relationship between AI adoption and sustainability imperatives in the field of legal education.

The assimilation of sustainability ethics into legal education amidst the adoption of AI marks a pivotal intersection of contemporary educational imperatives. As AI technologies permeate various sectors, including the legal domain, the imperative to infuse ethical considerations – particularly those pertaining to sustainability – becomes increasingly pronounced. The burgeoning presence of AI in the evolving landscape of legal education necessitates a conscientious integration of sustainability ethics to navigate the ethical challenges and seize the opportunities inherent in this technological shift. The adoption of AI in legal education represents a transformative paradigm shift, promising enhanced efficiency, accessibility and innovation in pedagogical approaches and legal practice. AI-driven tools offer students and practitioners unprecedented capabilities in legal research, document analysis and case management, revolutionising traditional modes of legal education and practice.[5] However, amidst this rapid technological advancement, questions

---

4 K. Biedenweg, M. C. Monroe and A. Oxarart, 'The Importance of Teaching Ethics of Sustainability' (2013) 14 *International Journal of Sustainability in Higher Education* 6.
5 W. Wang, 'An Analysis of the Feasibility of Artificial Intelligence to Replace Lawyers' (2023) 6(2) *Advances in Politics and Economics* 161.

surrounding sustainability and ethics emerge as pivotal considerations that require careful scrutiny.

The implications of AI adoption in legal education extend beyond just pedagogical enhancement; they encompass profound ethical and sustainability dimensions. Concerns arise regarding equitable access to AI-driven resources, the preservation of data privacy and the mitigation of AI biases. Moreover, the ethical dilemmas posed by AI technologies – such as the potential for algorithmic discrimination and the erosion of human-centric legal practices – underscore the imperative for a robust framework of sustainability ethics within legal education. Against this backdrop, this book endeavours to explore the complicated intersection of AI adoption, sustainability ethics and legal education. By examining the evolving role of AI in legal education and its implications for sustainability and ethics, this study aims to elucidate the challenges and opportunities inherent in this technological convergence. Through a critical analysis of the ethical dimensions of AI adoption and a consideration of sustainable practices, this book seeks to offer insights into fostering a more ethical and sustainable approach to legal education in the era of AI. In terms of the intersection of sustainability, AI ethics and legal education this book is therefore focused on a specific ethics theme: that of an exploration of the ethical implications of AI adoption in legal education, with a particular emphasis on sustainability ethics in the UK context.

Sustainability and Legal Education

The relationship between sustainability and legal education is multi-layered and increasingly important in today's world. Sustainability refers to the capacity to meet the needs of the present without compromising the ability of future generations to meet their own needs.[6] Legal education plays a critical role in preparing lawyers to address environmental issues. The possibilities of incorporating an environmental sustainability perspective into the law curriculum at universities in England have been highlighted, as has the growing importance of environmental sustainability issues and the need for legal professionals to be well-versed in this field.[7] In this section, some key aspects of the relationship between sustainability and legal education will be outlined.

Environmental law is a specialised field that focuses on the legal aspects of environmental protection, conservation and sustainable resource management. Law schools often offer courses and programmes in environmental law to train lawyers in this area. However, moving beyond limiting sustainability

---

6 S. Holdsworth and I. Thomas, 'A Sustainability Education Academic Development Framework (SEAD)' (2016) 22 *Environmental Education Research* 1073.
7 D. M. Ong, 'Prospects for Integrating an Environmental Sustainability Perspective within the University Law Curriculum in England' (2016) 50 *The Law Teacher* 276.

to environmental law, legal education institutions have a significant role to play in advancing sustainability principles across a broad spectrum, including social, economic and cultural dimensions. The university sector, in general, has been discussing education for sustainable development since at least 2009, with the UK's Advance Higher Education being a notable advocate.[8] This underscores the fact that sustainability is not a new conversation in academia and that it has long been recognised as a core element of university missions to foster ethical and informed global citizens. Law schools, as centres for training future legal professionals, should see sustainability as a framework for guiding ethical decision-making, not just in environmental law cases but across a wide range of legal disciplines.

Sustainable development is a global goal, and legal professionals are instrumental in shaping policies and regulations that promote sustainable practices. Legal education can include coursework on international law, trade law and human rights law, which are all relevant to sustainable development. Businesses have a significant impact on sustainability. Legal education can prepare lawyers to advise companies on sustainable business practices, including compliance with environmental regulations, responsible sourcing and corporate social responsibility (CSR).[9] Significantly, sustainability is emerging as a key consideration for law firms and legal departments, as identified by Ernst & Young,[10] reflecting broader societal trends towards environmental responsibility and ethical business practices. This highlights the growing demand for legal professionals who understand how sustainability intersects with issues of justice, equity and corporate ethics.

From implementing green initiatives and reducing carbon footprints to promoting social responsibility and ethical governance, there is therefore a growing emphasis on incorporating sustainability principles into legal operations. Reflecting this, legal education can empower future lawyers to advocate for sustainability and environmental protection. Environmental law clinics and advocacy programmes within law schools can provide students with practical experience in advocating for environmental causes. Lawyers often play a key role in drafting, interpreting and enforcing regulations related to sustainability. Legal education can prepare students to work in government agencies or as legal advisers to policymakers in crafting laws and regulations

---

8 M. Grant, 'Education for Sustainable Development and Employability' (*Advance Higher Education*, 2009) <www.advance-he.ac.uk/knowledge-hub/education-sustainable-development-and-employability>.

9 United Nations Industrial Development Organisation, 'What is CSR? | UNIDO' (2023) www.unido.org/our-focus/advancing-economic-competitiveness/competitive-trade-capacities-and-corporate-responsibility/corporate-social-responsibility-market-integration/what-csr.

10 Ernst & Young Global Ltd, 'The General Counsel Imperative: How the Law Department is Key in Unlocking Your Sustainability Strategy' (2024) www.ey.com/en_gl/insights/law/how-the-law-department-is-key-in-unlocking-your-sustainability-strategy.

that promote sustainability. Some law schools and legal clinics engage with their communities to address sustainability issues at the local level. This can include providing legal assistance to environmental organisations, participating in community sustainability projects and educating the public about legal rights and responsibilities related to sustainability.

Many contemporary sustainability challenges require a multi-disciplinary approach – Ong emphasises the importance of interdisciplinary collaboration and the use of practical case studies and experiential learning to engage students in the subject matter.[11] Legal education can encourage collaboration with other fields – such as environmental science, engineering and economics – to develop holistic solutions to sustainability problems. Sustainability often involves ethical questions related to equity, justice and the well-being of future generations. Legal education can encourage students to explore these ethical dimensions and consider them in their practice. Legal academics and researchers can contribute to the body of knowledge related to sustainability by conducting research on legal frameworks, case studies and policy evaluations. The relationship between sustainability and legal education is thus significant and growing. Legal education equips future lawyers with the knowledge and skills needed to address environmental, social and economic sustainability challenges, both through their professional practice and their engagement with broader societal issues.

AI and Legal Education

The relationship between AI and legal education is evolving rapidly as technology continues to affect the legal profession. AI technologies such as ChatGPT are reshaping legal education by providing innovative tools for research, learning and practice.[12] Key aspects of this relationship include curriculum integration, AI-assisted legal research, practice simulations, legal tech competitions, ethical considerations, research opportunities, AI in legal clinics, continuing legal education, AI ethics and policy, and AI and access to justice.

Legal education institutions in the UK are increasingly embedding AI-related topics into their curricula.[13] This includes courses on AI and the law, legal tech and data privacy.[14] These courses help students understand the implications of AI for legal practice and the legal system. AI-powered tools

---

11 Ong (n 7).
12 M. Ajevski, K. Barker, A. Gilbert, L. Hardie and F. Ryan, 'ChatGPT and the Future of Legal Education and Practice' (2023) *The Law Teacher* 1.
13 V. N. Enebeli, 'Artificial Intelligence and The Future of Legal Education: Lessons from The United Kingdom and South Africa' (2024) 15(1) *Journal of Education and Practice* 89.
14 F. Ryan and H. McFaul, 'Innovative Technologies in UK Legal Education' in E. Jones and F. Cownie (eds), *Key Directions in Legal Education National and International Perspectives* (Routledge, Abingdon 2020) 67–79.

6 *AI and Legal Education*

and platforms, such as legal research software, are becoming essential for legal professionals.[15] Law schools often provide training on how to use AI tools effectively for legal research and document review. Some law schools are incorporating AI-based practice simulations into their programmes.[16] These simulations provide students with opportunities to work with AI systems that mimic real legal scenarios, helping them gain practical experience. Many law schools host competitions related to legal technology and AI. These events encourage students to develop innovative legal tech solutions, fostering an entrepreneurial mindset.

The use of AI in law raises ethical and regulatory questions which other professional fields, such as medicine, are also engaging with currently.[17] Legal education must address these concerns, helping students understand the ethical implications of AI in legal practice and guiding them on how to navigate these challenges. Legal scholars and researchers are exploring the legal and ethical aspects of AI, including its impact on the legal profession and the justice system.[18] Law schools may provide resources and opportunities for students to engage in AI-related research. Some legal clinics are leveraging AI tools to improve efficiency and access to legal services. Law students who participate in these clinics may gain exposure to AI technologies in real-world legal practice. Many practicing lawyers are required to complete continuing legal education (CLE) credits.[19] CLE programmes increasingly offer courses on AI and its relevance to legal practice, ensuring that practicing lawyers stay informed about technological advancements.

While AI-powered tools offer significant benefits to legal education by improving efficiency and assisting in complex legal tasks, there is an ongoing debate about how reliance on such technology might compromise students' development of essential legal skills, such as critical thinking and analytical reasoning. As one recent study highlights,[20] the "dark side" of AI raises questions about how governance and human oversight mechanisms can adapt to the unknown challenges that AI introduces into the legal domain. Legal educators must therefore strike a careful balance, ensuring that students are

---

15 The Lawyer, 'Can AI Transform Legal Education?' (2023) www.thelawyer.com/can-ai-transform-legal-education/.
16 BPP Holdings Ltd, 'AI in Law: Technology in Legal Education and the Profession' (2023) www.bpp.com/insights/ai-in-law.
17 H. V. Goldstein and J. C. Goldstein, 'Artificial Intelligence Education in Medicine: Lessons from "Hidden Figures"' (2021) 43 *Medical Teacher* 1222.
18 D. Black, 'Can Artificial Intelligence Lawfully Draft Statements of Case? Lessons from *JK v MK* [2020] EWFC 2' (2022) 41(2) *Civil Justice Quarterly* 136.
19 Solicitors' Regulation Authority, 'Continuing Competence' (2022) <www.sra.org.uk/continuing-competence>.
20 P. Mikalef, K. Conboy, J. E. Lundstrom and A. Popovic, 'Thinking Responsibly about Responsible AI and 'the Dark Side' of AI' (2022) 31(3) *European Journal of Information Systems* 257.

trained not only in how to use AI tools but also in understanding the limitations of such tools and maintaining the human judgement necessary for legal practice.

As AI continues to raise questions about ethics and regulation,[21] legal education can contribute to the development of policies and guidelines related to AI use in the legal field. Legal education institutions are exploring how AI can be used to enhance access to justice by automating routine legal tasks and providing affordable legal assistance.[22] Students may be exposed to projects and initiatives focused on using AI for access to justice. The relationship between AI and legal education is one of adaptation and assimilation. As AI technologies become increasingly relevant to the legal profession, legal education institutions are incorporating AI-related topics, tools and practices into their programmes to ensure that law students and practicing lawyers are well prepared to navigate the changing landscape of the legal field. This integration is essential for fostering innovation, improving legal services and addressing ethical and regulatory challenges associated with AI.

AI Adoption in Legal Education: Trends, Challenges and Opportunities

There is a notable trend towards the integration of AI technologies into legal education institutions, with 33% now regularly using generative AI tools.[23] This integration encompasses various aspects, including AI-driven research tools, virtual assistants for student support and AI-enhanced learning platforms. Many legal education institutions are collaborating with legal tech companies to incorporate AI-driven solutions into their curriculum and research activities. These partnerships facilitate access to cutting-edge AI technologies and expertise, enabling institutions to stay abreast of industry developments. AI-powered adaptive learning platforms are gaining traction in legal education, offering personalised learning experiences tailored to individual student needs and learning styles. These platforms leverage machine learning (ML) algorithms to analyse student performance data and provide targeted feedback and resources.

The legal education landscape is undoubtedly undergoing significant change and AI certainly has the potential to revolutionise the way legal education is delivered and consumed. However, it is important to acknowledge

---

21 Law Society Gazette, 'A Matter of Trust' (2024) www.lawgazette.co.uk/features/a-matter-of-trust/5119168.book.
22 Thomson Reuters Practical Law, 'Preparing Lawyers for a Future with AI: Desk Ready, Set, Go!' (2023) https://uk.practicallaw.thomsonreuters.com/w-041-1255.
23 LexisNexis, 'Exploring the Growing Appetite for Legal AI' (2024) www.lexisnexis.co.uk/blog/future-of-law/explore-the-growing-appetite-for-legal-ai.

8 AI and Legal Education

that this transformation is still in its early stages. While some proclaim AI as the transformative force already reshaping legal education, the reality is more nuanced. While there are exciting possibilities, current adoption remains limited. Studies like the ongoing research of Dahl and colleagues on the use of large language models (LLMs) as legal analytic tools highlight the continuing unreliability of such AI, particularly in relation to legal hallucinations (responses from these models that are not consistent with legal facts).[24] While there is significant potential for AI to affect legal education, it is also fair to say that its transformative effects have yet to be fully realised.

While the widespread adoption of AI in legal education is still evolving, several promising tools and platforms are making strides. AI-powered research platforms like Westlaw Edge[25] and Lex Machina[26] can now scan vast legal databases, identifying relevant cases and statutes with a high degree of accuracy. Document review tools like Kira[27] and eDiscovery[28] can now sift through large amounts of documentation, highlighting key clauses, extracting vital information and identifying inconsistencies. Alternative dispute resolution (ADR) online platforms like Modria[29] simulate online negotiation environments where students can interact with AI-powered virtual characters representing opposing parties. Personalised learning platforms like AdaptiBar[30] utilise AI to personalise legal assessment preparation for students. Virtual assistants like LawBot[31] provide a legal chatbot that students can interact with to ask basic legal questions.

Although it is, of course, accepted that the purpose of legal education is not solely as preparation for professional practice, it is significant that AI technology is also affecting the legal profession, as highlighted in a recent report by KPMG.[32] Generative AI tools have the ability to rapidly ingest and summarise large volumes of documents, which can transform how legal professionals handle tasks. This technology is affecting around 11% of tasks within the legal profession, leading to changes in workflow and

---

24 M. Dahl, V. Magesh, M. Suzgun and D. E. Ho, 'Large Legal Fictions: Profiling Legal Hallucinations in Large Language Models' (2024) https://doi.org/10.48550/arXiv.2401.01301.
25 Thomson Reuters, 'Westlaw Edge' (2024) https://legal.thomsonreuters.com/en/products/westlaw-edge.
26 LexisNexis, 'LexMachina' (2024) https://lexmachina.com/.
27 Kira Inc, 'Kira Systems' (2024) https://kirasystems.com/.
28 Proofpoint, 'What is eDiscovery?' www.proofpoint.com/uk/threat-reference/e-discovery.
29 Tyler Technologies, 'Modria' (2024) https://cedr.modria.com/.
30 AdaptiGroup, 'AdaptiBar' (2024) www.adaptibar.com/.
31 F6s.com 'LawBot UK' (2024) www.f6s.com/company/lawbotuk#about.
32 KPMG LLP, '2023 KPMG Generative AI Survey' (2024) https://kpmg.com/us/en/books/2023/generative-artificial-intelligence-2023.html.

Introduction 9

job responsibilities. A survey conducted by LexisNexis[33] among more than 1,000 legal professionals in the UK indicates that the vast majority (95%) of respondents foresee a discernible impact of generative AI on the legal field. Of these, 38% anticipate a significant impact, while 11% believe it will be transformative. In 2023, the forefront of AI adoption was led by in-house lawyers in large corporations (currently at 17% usage), closely followed by small law firms (13%), large law firms (12%) and medium-sized practices (also at 12%, albeit with lower daily usage). However, the long-term perspective within the industry paints a different picture. LexisNexis also reports that a significant 64% of large law firms are actively exploring the implementation of generative AI, with in-house lawyers (47%), medium-sized practices (33%) and small firms (31%) trailing behind. The Bar (20%) and the public sector (14%) lag behind, with the former likely concerned about reputational risk and the latter potentially grappling with bureaucratic processes.

Despite the proliferation of AI technologies in legal education and practice, concerns persist regarding equitable access to these tools. Limited access to technology and digital literacy barriers may exacerbate existing disparities among students, undermining efforts to promote inclusivity and diversity in legal education. The use of AI-driven platforms in legal education raises concerns about data privacy and security. Institutions must ensure robust safeguards to protect sensitive student data from unauthorised access or misuse, adhering to stringent data protection regulations. Ethical considerations loom large in the adoption of AI technologies in legal education. Issues such as algorithmic bias, transparency, accountability and the ethical use of AI-generated content pose complex challenges that demand careful consideration and mitigation strategies.[34]

AI technologies have the potential to revolutionise legal education by facilitating immersive learning experiences, fostering critical thinking skills and providing real-time feedback to students. AI-powered simulations, case studies and interactive tutorials can enrich the learning process and better prepare students for legal practice. AI-driven tools offer opportunities for streamlining administrative tasks such as grading, document review and research, freeing up faculty time for more interactive and engaging teaching activities. Moreover, AI can catalyse innovation in legal education by enabling experimentation with new teaching methods and pedagogical approaches. The interdisciplinary nature of AI opens avenues for collaboration between legal

---

33 LexisNexis, 'Generative AI and the Future of the Legal Profession' (2024) www.lexisnexis. co.uk/insights/generative-ai-and-the-future-of-the-legal-profession/index.html.
34 Solicitors' Regulation Authority, 'Risk Outlook Report: The Use of Artificial Intelligence in the Legal Market' (2023) www.sra.org.uk/sra/research-publications/artificial-intelligence-legal-market/.

education institutions and other disciplines, such as computer science, data science and ethics. Joint initiatives can foster cross-disciplinary research, curriculum development and policy dialogue, enriching the educational experience and addressing complex societal challenges.

Overall, the transformational impact of AI on legal education is complex, with both promises and pitfalls. While AI technologies hold immense potential for enhancing learning outcomes, improving efficiency and fostering innovation, they also present challenges related to access, ethics and data privacy. By navigating these obstacles thoughtfully and leveraging the opportunities presented by AI, legal education institutions can adapt to the evolving landscape and prepare students for success in the digital age.

The Sustainability Challenges of Addressing the Impact of AI in Legal Education

Sustainability ethics encompasses principles and values aimed at promoting long-term well-being, equity and environmental stewardship for present and future generations.[35] In the context of legal education, sustainability ethics plays a crucial role in shaping the curriculum, institutional practices and ethical responsibilities of law schools. For example, AI in legal education often involves the collection and processing of sensitive data. Ensuring the privacy and security of this data is a sustainability challenge. The risk of data breaches and unauthorised access to sensitive information is a significant concern that goes beyond legal education.[36] Data breaches and unauthorised access can have legal, ethical and reputational consequences, affecting the sustainability of educational institutions. Institutions must therefore adhere diligently to relevant data protection regulations, such as the General Data Protection Regulation (GDPR) of the European Union (EU).[37] AI tools used in legal education may also have biases that can perpetuate social inequalities. Ensuring that AI systems are fair and do not discriminate against marginalised communities is crucial for promoting sustainability in terms of social justice and equity. Addressing the impact of AI in legal education while promoting sustainability can pose several other challenges, including environmental

---

35 D. Ofori-Sasu, G. N. A. Donkor and J. Y. Abor, 'Do Sustainability Ethics Explain the Impact of Country-Level Corporate Governance on Financial Stability in Developing Economies?' (2023) 13(4) *Journal of Sustainable Finance & Investment* 1415.
36 W. Luo, H. He, J. Liu, I. R. Berson, M. J. Berson, Y. Zhou and H. Li, 'Aladdin's Genie or Pandora's Box for Early Childhood Education? Experts Chat on the Roles, Challenges, and Developments of ChatGPT' (2023) *Early Education and Development* 1.
37 EUR-Lex, 'Regulation (EU) 2016/679' (2016) <http://data.europa.eu/eli/reg/2016/679>.

sustainability, social justice and equity, ethical decision-making and professional responsibility.

Law schools have a responsibility to promote environmental sustainability within their institutions and beyond. By integrating environmental law and sustainability principles into the curriculum, law schools can equip students with the knowledge and skills to address environmental challenges and advocate for sustainable practices in legal practice. But balancing the costs of AI implementation with other sustainability initiatives – such as reducing energy consumption or supporting diversity and inclusion – can be a complex task. Preparing faculty and staff to use AI tools and technologies effectively can be resource intensive and time consuming. Sustainable professional development programmes must be in place to ensure that educators can harness AI's potential while minimising disruptions and environmental impact.

Integrating ethical considerations into the curriculum is essential for preparing law students to navigate complex ethical dilemmas in legal practice. Sustainability ethics encourages critical reflection on the social, economic and environmental impacts of legal decisions and policies.[38] Law schools can incorporate case studies, discussions and experiential learning opportunities that explore the ethical dimensions of sustainability and environmental justice issues. Law schools have an obligation to instil ethical values and professional responsibility in their students. This includes fostering a commitment to sustainability, social responsibility and ethical conduct in legal practice. By embedding sustainability ethics into the curriculum, law schools can cultivate ethical leaders who value environmental protection, social justice and the public interest in their legal careers.

Sustainability ethics also encompasses principles of social justice and equity.[39] Law schools should strive to promote diversity, inclusion and access to legal education for all students, regardless of background or socioeconomic status. This entails creating inclusive learning environments, providing financial aid and support services, and addressing systemic barriers to participation in legal education. The adoption of AI in legal education may exacerbate the digital divide if students from disadvantaged backgrounds lack access to the necessary technology and internet connectivity. Bridging this divide and ensuring equal access to AI-driven educational resources is a sustainability challenge. Addressing the ethical implications of AI in legal education is also vital for sustainability. Ensuring that AI is used in ways that align with ethical

---

38 E. P. Metzger and R. R. Curren, 'Sustainability: Why the Language and Ethics of Sustainability Matter in the Geoscience Classroom' (2017) 65(2) *Journal of Geoscience Education* 93.
39 D. Zwarthoed, 'Why Sustainability Principles should Integrate Global Justice Concerns' (2017) 20(3) *Ethics, Policy & Environment* 251.

principles and legal standards requires ongoing vigilance and adaptation of educational practices.

While the primary lens for addressing equity concerns may be social justice, there is a link to sustainability in that equitable access contributes to the long-term viability of AI as a tool for all learners. Without addressing equity, the implementation of AI in education could exacerbate existing inequalities, leaving marginalised groups further disadvantaged. This would undermine the broader sustainability of AI as an inclusive and universally beneficial tool, especially in legal education where access to knowledge and resources is essential for producing competent and socially responsible legal professionals. For example, if AI resources are disproportionately accessible to wealthier or more privileged students, this inequitable distribution could lead to a widening educational gap, ultimately affecting the sustainability of the legal profession itself. Ensuring that all learners have equal access to AI-driven tools is essential for maintaining the long-term relevance and fairness of legal education and for fostering a legal profession that serves all segments of society.

In summary, sustainability ethics is highly relevant to legal education, guiding law schools in promoting environmental sustainability, social justice and ethical decision-making among students and faculty. By incorporating sustainability principles into the curriculum and institutional practices, law schools can fulfil their ethical responsibilities and contribute to a more just, equitable and sustainable legal profession and society. To address these sustainability challenges, legal education institutions should develop comprehensive AI strategies that consider environmental impact, data privacy, equity, ethics and long-term sustainability. Collaborations among institutions, government agencies and industry partners can also help create guidelines and best practices for sustainable AI adoption in legal education.

The Connections Between Ethics, Sustainability and AI in Legal Education

In view of the preceding discussion, this section aims to set out a theoretical framework that provides a basis for understanding the ethical implications of AI adoption in legal education and underscores the importance of incorporating sustainability considerations into AI-driven educational practices. There are connections among sustainability, ethics and AI in legal education, although they may not be immediately obvious. AI raises ethical questions related to bias, fairness and transparency. Sustainable AI in legal education may involve discussions about the ethical implications of using AI in decision-making processes, particularly those related to sustainability and environmental justice. Most importantly, by assimilating sustainability ethics and AI ethics into legal education, institutions can cultivate a culture of ethical awareness, social responsibility and environmental stewardship among students and practitioners.

Sustainability ethics encompasses principles and values aimed at promoting the long-term well-being of individuals, communities and the environment. Rooted in the concept of sustainable development, sustainability ethics emphasises the responsible stewardship of resources, the equitable distribution of benefits and burdens, and the preservation of ecological integrity for present and future generations.[40] Central to sustainability ethics are considerations of justice, equity, intergenerational equity and ecological resilience. AI ethics pertains to the ethical principles and guidelines governing the design, development, deployment and use of AI technologies.[41] Key ethical considerations in AI include transparency, fairness, accountability, privacy, autonomy and bias mitigation. AI ethics seeks to ensure that AI systems uphold fundamental human values, respect human rights and contribute to societal well-being, while minimising harm and unintended consequences.

The tension between conventional AI ethics and sustainability in AI development arises from differing priorities and objectives within these two domains. Conventional AI ethics focuses primarily on principles such as fairness, transparency, accountability and privacy, which are designed to address issues such as algorithmic bias, discrimination and the ethical implications of AI decision-making processes. While conventional AI ethics aims to ensure that AI systems are developed and deployed in a manner that respects fundamental human rights and values, it may not explicitly prioritise environmental sustainability as a core consideration. Sustainability in AI development encompasses considerations related to the environmental impact of AI technologies, including energy consumption, carbon emissions and resource depletion.[42] Sustainable AI development aims to minimise the environmental footprint of AI systems throughout their life cycle, from design and manufacturing to usage and disposal. However, sustainability considerations such as energy efficiency, renewable resources and waste reduction may not always align with traditional AI ethics principles or prioritise ethical concerns over environmental impacts.

The tension between conventional AI ethics and sustainability in AI development therefore arises when ethical considerations – such as fairness and transparency – conflict with sustainability goals such as data protection,

---

40 D. A. Fennell, 'Sustainability Ethics in Tourism: The Imperative Next Imperative' (2019) 44(1) *Tourism Recreation Research* 117.
41 J. Rogers and F. Bell, 'The Ethical AI Lawyer: What is Required of Lawyers When They Use Automated Systems?' (2019) 1 *Law, Technology and Humans* 80.
42 A. van Wynsberghe, 'Sustainable AI: AI for Sustainability and the Sustainability of AI' (2021) 1 *AI Ethics* 213.

limiting energy consumption or reducing electronic waste. Optimising AI algorithms for fairness and accuracy may require complex calculations and high computational resources, leading to increased energy consumption and environmental impact. Additionally, emphasising privacy and data protection may result in the duplication of data storage and processing, further exacerbating sustainability challenges. AI systems increasingly rely on vast amounts of data to function effectively. This dependence on large datasets creates significant challenges for data privacy as more personal, sensitive or proprietary information is collected, processed and stored. As AI systems grow, the sheer volume of data collected presents additional risks such as data breaches, loss of control over personal information and increased surveillance, all of which have long-term ethical and societal implications.

When considering sustainability in AI, it is therefore crucial to evaluate not only the environmental impact of technologies but also how AI influences societal structures, individual freedoms and rights, including privacy. In this sense, data privacy becomes a sustainability issue because it deals with the long-term implications of how personal data is used, stored and shared within AI systems. The failure to protect data privacy could have enduring consequences for individuals and societies, thereby challenging the sustainability of AI practices. As noted previously, while social justice concerns – such as equity in access to technology – are often seen as distinct from environmental sustainability, they intersect in important ways when considering the long-term societal impacts of AI. Sustainability is not just about preserving the environment but also about promoting equitable access and social justice for future generations. Data privacy plays a critical role in this intersection, as marginalised groups are often affected disproportionately by data misuse, surveillance and inequitable access to technology. Addressing the ethical implications of data usage in AI systems is thus essential for creating sustainable and equitable technological solutions.

The literature on sustainable AI explores strategies and frameworks for developing and deploying AI technologies in a manner that aligns with sustainability goals. Hallenberg and Haddow emphasise the interconnected nature of sustainability issues, including environmental, social and economic aspects.[43] Similarly, addressing the impact of AI in legal education requires an understanding of how AI intersects with legal, ethical and societal dimensions, making the interconnectedness of these issues relevant. This includes decreasing the environmental footprint of AI infrastructure, promoting energy efficiency and leveraging AI for sustainable development initiatives. Sustainable AI also encompasses considerations of social and economic sustainability, such as addressing digital divides, promoting

---

[43] K. M. Hallenberg and C. Haddow, 'Beyond Criminal Justice: Connecting Justice and Sustainability' (2016) 50 *The Law Teacher* 352.

inclusivity and mitigating the negative impacts of AI on employment and social cohesion.

The adoption of AI technologies in educational settings raises ethical considerations related to pedagogy, privacy, equity and autonomy. In legal education, AI-driven tools may influence teaching methods, assessment practices and student engagement, presenting both opportunities and challenges. Ethical questions arise regarding the transparency of AI algorithms used in educational platforms, the protection of student data privacy and the potential for AI to perpetuate or exacerbate existing inequalities in access to education and resources. In legal education, the intersection of sustainability, ethics and AI manifests in various ways. Sustainability ethics informs decisions about the adoption and use of AI technologies in legal education, guiding institutions to prioritise environmentally sustainable AI solutions and ethical AI practices. Ethical considerations shape the design and implementation of AI-driven pedagogical tools, ensuring that they adhere to principles of fairness, transparency and accountability.

Moreover, AI technologies offer opportunities to embed sustainability and ethics into the legal curriculum, facilitating interdisciplinary approaches to environmental law, social justice and ethical decision-making. Legal scholars and researchers have already explored the intersection of ethics, AI and the law.[44] In the future, this could include researching legal frameworks for AI-driven sustainable practices, the use of AI in climate change mitigation and the legal implications of AI-powered green technologies. Legal education can foster entrepreneurship by supporting students in creating legal tech start-ups focused on sustainability and AI. These start-ups may develop innovative solutions for legal professionals and organisations engaged in sustainability efforts. Ultimately, sustainability and AI intersect in legal education through various avenues, including discussions on AI's environmental impact, the development of sustainable AI policies and regulations, and the application of AI to address environmental challenges. Legal education can play a crucial role in preparing future lawyers to navigate the legal, ethical and practical aspects of AI in the context of sustainability and environmental protection, and this is what will be considered next.

The Role of Law Schools in Addressing Ethical Sustainability Challenges Related to AI Adoption

As previously noted, law schools play a pivotal role in addressing ethical sustainability challenges related to AI adoption by equipping future legal

---

44 A. Zuckerman, 'Artificial Intelligence – Implications for the Legal Profession, Adversarial Process and Rule of Law' (2020) 136(Jul) *Law Quarterly Review* 427.

professionals with the knowledge, skills and ethical awareness needed to navigate the complex intersection of AI, sustainability and law. For example, law schools can introduce courses on AI law, ethics and sustainability into their curriculum to educate students about the legal and ethical implications of AI adoption. However, it is crucial to recognise the various "push and pull" factors faced by law schools, which may influence their approach to AI. Universities often prioritise sustainability objectives and have established policies for energy efficiency and resource management, which might push law schools towards adopting sustainable AI solutions. Law firms and other legal employers increasingly value graduates with AI literacy and proficiency in working with AI tools. This pull factor might incentivise law schools to integrate AI into their curricula, even if there are sustainability concerns. However, limited budgets and infrastructure limitations in law schools can be a significant push factor against widespread adoption of resource-intensive AI tools.

Furthermore, it is important to acknowledge that law schools may not have complete control over the pace and direction of AI integration. Universities may make centralised decisions on cloud computing resources and data centres, potentially affecting the sustainability of AI tools used by law schools. Legal professional bodies and employers might have specific requirements for the type of legal education graduates receive, e.g., in light of the advent of the Solicitors' Qualifying Examination (SQE), affecting the flexibility for law schools to experiment with AI-powered learning methods. By understanding the pull and push factors within the ecosystem, law schools can fulfil their responsibilities to integrate AI in a responsible and sustainable manner. Collaboration, strategic leadership and a focus on critical thinking skills are key for law schools to navigate this complex landscape. They can influence the broader conversation on AI in legal education, advocating for sustainable solutions that benefit all stakeholders, including students, the profession and the environment. Overcoming the sustainability challenges associated with the impact of AI in legal education requires a combination of strategies and interventions.

In the following chapters are some approaches that educational institutions and stakeholders can implement. Introducing these strategies and interventions requires a holistic and coordinated approach involving multiple stakeholders, including administrators, faculty, students and external partners. Continuous monitoring and adaptation are essential to ensure that AI adoption in legal education aligns with sustainability goals and values. Chapter 1 explores how law schools can promote ethical AI practices that align with sustainability goals and values. Chapter 2 investigates the sustainability implications of AI biases in legal education and strategies to address these biases. Chapter 3 looks at measures institutions can implement to mitigate the digital divide in AI-driven legal education and sustain digital inclusion initiatives over time. Chapter 4 examines the crucial role sustainable faculty development programmes play in ensuring the long-term viability of AI initiatives in legal education. Chapter 5 considers the intricate challenge faced by law schools to stay vigilant and proactive in addressing the evolving landscape of AI-related regulations and ethical standards. Chapter 6 discusses the sustainability challenges related to data privacy and security in AI-driven legal education and how to address them. Chapter 7 analyses the long-term viability of AI solutions in legal education and strategies to address this aspect of sustainability effectively.

1 Ethical Considerations in AI Adoption

Ethical considerations are of paramount importance in the adoption of AI in legal education and are integral to ensuring sustainability. Ajevski and colleagues highlight the ethical considerations associated with AI in the legal field.[1] Sustainability challenges often involve ethical dimensions, such as the environmental impact of AI. Educating legal professionals about these ethical dimensions and their role in addressing them is relevant to sustainability efforts. Ethical principles guide how AI is used, safeguarding the rights and well-being of students, educators and the broader legal community. AI technologies, while offering significant potential to revolutionise legal education, also pose risks related to bias, privacy, transparency and accessibility. Legal education institutions have a responsibility to guide future professionals in understanding these ethical dimensions and in integrating AI in a manner that promotes both ethical conduct and long-term sustainability. The ethical implications of AI go beyond mere technical challenges; they touch on fundamental principles of justice, fairness and human rights. As legal professionals are increasingly likely to use AI tools in their practice, their education must include a strong foundation in the ethical use of these technologies. This also ties into broader discussions of sustainability, as ethical AI practices ensure that legal education remains inclusive, fair and equitable over the long term.

The adoption of AI in legal education presents several ethical sustainability challenges. These challenges need to be addressed to ensure that AI use aligns with sustainability goals and ethical values. Integrating AI into legal education necessitates curriculum adjustments to cover AI-related topics, ethical considerations and the environmental impact of AI technology.[2] AI systems often process vast amounts of personal and sensitive data, particularly in educational settings. The ethical obligation

---

1 M. Ajevski, K. Barker, A. Gilbert, L. Hardie and F. Ryan, 'ChatGPT and the Future of Legal Education and Practice' (2023) *The Law Teacher* 1.
2 D. M. Ong, 'Prospects for Integrating an Environmental Sustainability Perspective within the University Law Curriculum in England' (2016) 50 *The Law Teacher* 276.

DOI: 10.4324/9781003607397-2

to protect student data is paramount. Institutions must ensure robust data privacy measures and comply with legal standards, such as the GDPR, to protect against misuse or unauthorised access to student information. AI algorithms, when not carefully designed, can perpetuate biases present in the data on which they are trained. These biases can manifest in assessments, recommendations or other AI-driven educational tools, potentially disadvantaging certain student groups based on race, gender or socioeconomic status. Mitigating bias is an ethical imperative to ensure fairness and equity in AI applications. AI systems can make decisions in ways that are opaque or difficult to understand. Ethical AI adoption requires transparency in how algorithms function, providing students and educators with insight into the logic behind AI-generated recommendations or outcomes. This transparency is critical to maintaining trust in AI technologies and ensuring that AI tools are used responsibly. Ensuring that AI systems and resources are accessible to all students, including those with disabilities or from underserved communities, is another key ethical consideration. Inclusive AI design ensures that the benefits of AI are equitably distributed, fostering a more just and accessible educational environment. Questions about the ownership of AI-generated content, tools or research outputs also raise ethical and legal issues. Law schools must establish clear guidelines on intellectual property rights and ensure that both students and faculty understand the ethical and legal implications of using AI in their work.

Law schools can promote ethical AI practices that align with sustainability goals and values using the following strategies.

1.1 AI Ethics Committees and Review Boards

AI ethics committees or review boards composed of experts in AI, ethics, education and legal practice can serve as oversight mechanisms to evaluate the ethical implications of AI use in education. Ethics committees assess the ethical dimensions of AI initiatives, including data privacy, bias, transparency and inclusivity. They review proposed AI applications and provide guidance on potential ethical concerns. These committees offer continuous oversight, ensuring that AI practices remain aligned with ethical standards and values as technology evolves. AI ethics committees and review boards play a crucial role in ensuring the responsible and ethical use of AI technologies in education, especially in fields like legal education where issues of fairness, transparency and privacy are paramount. These bodies, composed of a diverse group of experts in AI, ethics, education and legal practice, serve as essential oversight mechanisms. Their primary responsibility is to evaluate the ethical implications of AI adoption and use within institutions, ensuring that practices adhere to both current ethical standards and long-term sustainability goals.

1.1.1 Composition of AI Ethics Committees

AI ethics committees typically consist of a multi-disciplinary group of stakeholders, including AI experts (technologists who understand the technical functioning of AI systems, including ML, algorithm development and data processing); ethicists (professionals who specialise in the moral implications of technology, privacy and fairness, ensuring that AI use aligns with societal values); legal practitioners (lawyers and legal scholars who focus on the regulatory and legal aspects of AI use, including compliance with data protection laws, intellectual property rights and emerging AI-related legislation); and educators and pedagogical experts (individuals who are responsible for designing and delivering AI-integrated curricula, ensuring that AI enhances, rather than detracts from, the learning process). This diverse composition ensures a holistic review of AI practices, considering technical, ethical, legal and educational dimensions. The interdisciplinary nature of the committee helps to bridge gaps between technical capabilities and human-centric ethical considerations.

1.1.2 Responsibilities of AI Ethics Committees

AI ethics committees are responsible for assessing the ethical dimensions of AI initiatives in education. Some key responsibilities include evaluating data privacy concerns, addressing algorithmic bias, ensuring transparency, promoting inclusivity and assessing long-term ethical impacts. AI systems often process large amounts of sensitive student data, including performance metrics, learning habits and personal information. Ethics committees ensure that data privacy laws, such as GDPR or California Consumer Privacy Act (CCPA), are adhered to and that proper safeguards are in place to protect student data from unauthorised access or misuse. This includes assessing whether data collection practices are transparent and obtaining informed consent from students. AI tools used in legal education, such as automated grading systems or AI-driven research tools, can unintentionally perpetuate biases that exist in the data they are trained on. Committees are tasked with scrutinising these tools for potential bias and recommending strategies to mitigate such risks. For example, they may advise developers on how to adjust training datasets to avoid reinforcing stereotypes or unfair outcomes for certain student groups. AI algorithms often operate as "black boxes," making it difficult for users to understand how decisions are made. Committees push for greater transparency, ensuring that students, educators and administrators have insight into how AI-driven systems function. This is especially important in legal education, where understanding the reasoning behind decisions is critical to fostering trust in AI technologies. The committee ensures that AI tools and systems are accessible to all students, regardless of their socioeconomic background, abilities or prior experience with technology. Inclusive AI systems promote equity, making sure that students from underrepresented groups are not left behind in AI-driven learning environments. Beyond immediate concerns, committees also examine the long-term ethical and societal impacts of adopting AI in education. This includes considerations about the environmental sustainability of AI systems, as well as the broader ethical issues related to job displacement, the role of AI in the legal profession and the ethical training of future legal professionals.

1.1.3 Continuous Oversight and Monitoring

One of the primary functions of AI ethics committees is to provide continuous oversight of AI initiatives. As technology evolves, new ethical challenges may arise, and AI systems that are deemed ethically sound today may require reassessment in the future. Continuous monitoring allows institutions to stay agile in responding to new risks, adapting AI systems and policies as necessary. Ethics committees should conduct regular evaluations of AI systems and policies. This could include annual audits of AI tools, with a focus on data handling practices, algorithmic fairness and compliance with updated laws or ethical standards. AI technology evolves rapidly, often outpacing existing ethical frameworks. Ethics committees must stay informed about technological advances, ensuring that new AI tools, such as generative AI or more sophisticated ML models, are subject to the same rigorous ethical review as earlier systems.

1.1.4 Providing Guidance and Recommendations

In addition to oversight, AI ethics committees provide proactive guidance to institutions looking to adopt or expand their use of AI technologies. This may include developing ethical AI policies, training and education, and advising on ethical dilemmas. The committee can assist in drafting or revising institutional policies related to the ethical use of AI, ensuring that these policies align with best practices in both education and AI governance. AI ethics committees can also play a role in educating faculty, administrators and students about the ethical dimensions of AI use. This could involve creating training programmes that emphasise data ethics, algorithmic transparency and responsible AI use in legal education. As ethical issues arise, committees act as advisers, helping to navigate complex dilemmas related to AI use. For instance, if a faculty member raises concerns about bias in an AI grading tool, the committee can investigate the issue and recommend solutions.

The establishment of AI ethics committees offers several benefits to legal education institutions, including safeguarding student rights, building trust in AI systems, enhancing ethical AI education and supporting sustainability goals. By scrutinising data privacy and AI fairness, ethics committees help protect students' rights and well-being. Transparent AI practices foster trust among students and faculty, encouraging wider adoption of AI tools. By integrating ethical considerations into the AI adoption process, committees ensure that future legal professionals are trained to understand and navigate the ethical challenges posed by AI in their field. Continuous oversight ensures that AI systems are aligned with long-term sustainability goals, including environmental considerations and the responsible use of resources. AI ethics committees and review boards are critical to ensuring the responsible and ethical use of AI in legal education. By providing continuous oversight; evaluating ethical dimensions such as data privacy, bias and inclusivity; and offering guidance on the adoption of AI technologies, these committees ensure that AI practices align with institutional values and societal expectations. They play a key role in building a sustainable and ethically sound AI ecosystem in legal education.

1.2 AI Ethics Guidelines and Policies

Comprehensive AI ethics guidelines and policies that are tailored to the specific needs and values of the legal education institution can serve as a framework for ethical AI use. Guidelines should stipulate the importance of explaining how AI algorithms arrive at their conclusions and include provisions that emphasise transparency in AI decision-making processes. Outlining protocols for data collection, storage and protection addresses data privacy concerns. Ethics policies should emphasise the mitigation of biases in AI systems and ensure compliance with relevant data protection regulations, such as GDPR. Institutions should proactively work to ensure fairness in AI-generated educational content and assessments. Comprehensive AI ethics guidelines and policies are critical in legal education, ensuring the ethical deployment and use of AI technologies in academic and administrative contexts. These guidelines not only provide a framework for addressing ethical concerns but also align AI use with the values, needs and legal responsibilities of educational institutions. By creating a robust and transparent system, institutions can foster trust, accountability and fairness in the application of AI tools. What follows is an overview of the key elements and strategies involved in formulating AI ethics guidelines and policies tailored to legal education.

1.2.1 Tailoring Guidelines to Institutional Values

AI ethics guidelines should be closely aligned with the core mission, values and priorities of the legal education institution. For law schools and legal education institutions, where justice, fairness and equity are fundamental values, the ethical use of AI technologies must reflect these principles. This means guidelines should promote access to justice, support professional ethics and foster critical engagement with AI. In line with the legal profession's commitment to fairness and equality, AI systems used in legal education should enhance equitable access to educational resources, rather than exacerbate existing disparities. AI systems used in legal education must also be guided by the principles that define the legal profession, including confidentiality, due process and respect for individual rights. Law students must not only learn how to use AI tools but also how to critically examine their implications for the legal system. Ethics guidelines should emphasise the importance of educating students about AI's impact on society, including ethical and legal challenges.

1.2.2 Transparency in AI Decision-Making

One of the foundational principles of AI ethics is transparency. AI-driven decision-making processes – whether used in grading, admissions or legal research – must be explainable and understandable to students, faculty and administrators. To ensure transparency, ethics guidelines should include provisions for explainability, auditability and user-friendly interfaces. AI systems should be designed so that the reasoning behind their outputs is clear. In a legal education context, this is particularly important, as students and educators need to understand the logic behind AI-driven recommendations, such as automated grading or legal analysis tools. The guidelines should ensure that AI models are equipped with mechanisms to explain how specific outcomes are generated. Institutions must have the capacity to audit AI systems to verify their performance and fairness. Auditability ensures that the institution can track the decision-making process of AI systems, providing a mechanism for accountability if biases or errors are detected. AI tools should present information in a way that is accessible to non-experts. Legal educators and students should not need to possess deep technical knowledge to understand how an AI system operates. User interfaces should include features that clearly outline AI processes and decisions in simple terms.

1.2.3 Data Privacy and Protection

Data privacy is an essential concern when incorporating AI technologies into legal education. AI systems often rely on large volumes of personal data to operate effectively, making it crucial that institutions take steps to safeguard student, faculty and institutional data. Comprehensive AI ethics guidelines must outline strict protocols for data collection, storage, and protection, including compliance with data protection regulations, data minimisation and secure data storage. Legal education institutions must ensure that their AI systems comply with relevant data protection laws, such as the GDPR in Europe or the CCPA in the United States. Compliance involves adhering to strict standards on how personal data is collected, used and stored, including obtaining consent from data subjects and ensuring that data is not used for purposes outside the original intent. Institutions should adopt the principle of data minimisation, ensuring that only the necessary amount of personal data is collected and used by AI systems. This reduces the risk of privacy violations while also minimising the institution's legal liability. AI ethics policies must include specific guidelines for storing personal data securely. This could involve encrypting data, restricting access to sensitive information and implementing protocols for data anonymisation, ensuring that personal data cannot be traced back to individual students or faculty.

1.2.4 Mitigating Bias in AI Systems

AI systems often rely on historical data, which can contain biases reflecting societal inequities. If not properly addressed, these biases can be perpetuated and even amplified by AI algorithms. In a legal education context, where fairness and impartiality are core values, it is critical to mitigate biases in AI-generated educational content, assessments and research tools. Ethics policies should address this by bias detection and mitigation protocols, fairness in AI assessments and inclusive AI development. AI ethics guidelines must require regular bias testing in AI systems, with specific protocols for identifying and addressing biases. This includes examining training data for potential biases related to race, gender, socioeconomic background or other protected characteristics. AI-driven assessment tools, such as automated essay scoring systems, should be regularly reviewed for fairness. Legal education institutions must ensure that AI grading systems do not unfairly disadvantage students from diverse backgrounds. For instance, AI-driven assessments should not reflect biases present in the training data, such as favouring specific linguistic or writing styles. Involving diverse teams in the development and oversight of AI systems can help mitigate biases. Institutions should encourage the participation of individuals from varied backgrounds in AI governance, including faculty, students and external experts, to provide a range of perspectives on the fairness of AI systems.

1.2.5 Compliance With Intellectual Property Laws

As AI-generated content becomes more prevalent, issues surrounding intellectual property (IP) rights arise. Legal education institutions must ensure that AI-generated content – whether it be research papers, legal briefs or instructional materials – does not infringe upon existing copyright laws. AI ethics guidelines should include clear ownership guidelines, copyright compliance and addressing AI-generated works. Institutions should establish clear rules regarding ownership of AI-generated content. For example, if an AI system assists a student or faculty member in generating content, the guidelines should

Ethical Considerations in AI Adoption 25

clarify who owns the IP rights to that content. Law schools must ensure that AI tools used in legal education do not inadvertently violate copyright laws by reproducing or generating content based on copyrighted material without proper authorisation. Institutions should implement mechanisms to verify the originality of AI-generated content and prevent plagiarism. As AI systems are increasingly capable of generating original legal content, such as case briefs or memos, institutions must address how these AI-generated works fit within existing IP frameworks. Ethics policies should clarify whether these works are eligible for copyright protection and, if so, who retains ownership – the AI developer, the user or the institution.

1.2.6 Proactive Fairness and Compliance Initiatives

Legal education institutions should not wait for issues to arise before implementing ethical AI practices. Instead, they should take proactive steps to ensure fairness, transparency and compliance in all AI-related activities. Some strategies include pre-emptive bias audits, ethics training for faculty and students, and periodic policy reviews. Regularly conducting bias audits of AI systems before they are deployed ensures that any fairness issues are addressed early on. Institutions can work with external auditors to evaluate the fairness of their AI systems and identify areas for improvement. Law schools must provide ongoing training for faculty and students on the ethical implications of AI use in legal education. This training should cover topics such as data privacy, bias mitigation and the responsible use of AI-generated content. Educating users about the potential risks and benefits of AI tools can help foster a culture of ethical awareness within the institution. Given the rapid evolution of AI technologies, AI ethics guidelines should be reviewed and updated regularly to ensure that they remain relevant and effective. Institutions should establish a committee or task force responsible for overseeing these updates and ensuring compliance with the latest ethical standards and regulations.

AI ethics guidelines and policies are essential to fostering responsible, transparent and fair AI use in legal education. By addressing key concerns such as data privacy, bias mitigation, transparency and compliance with IP laws, these guidelines ensure that AI technologies are integrated in a manner that aligns with the core values of the legal profession and the institution. Through proactive initiatives, continuous oversight and regular updates, legal education institutions can create an AI ecosystem that promotes ethical innovation, protects student rights and enhances the overall quality and fairness of legal education.

1.3 Open Ethical Discussions

Institutions should foster a culture that encourages open discussions on ethical dilemmas related to AI among students and faculty, create a safe space for dialogues on the ethical implications of AI adoption and integrate discussions on AI ethics into the curriculum. Students should be encouraged to examine the ethical dimensions of AI use in legal practice and education critically. Lim and Allan highlight the role of scenarios in preparing future legal professionals to address sustainability challenges by considering potential legal issues and solutions in dynamic contexts.[3] Scenario-based learning can also encourage students to engage in ethical reasoning and consider the ethical implications of AI technologies. Organising seminars, workshops and guest speaker sessions on AI ethics, inviting experts to engage with the legal education community and share insights on ethical considerations, and raising awareness about the importance of AI ethics through campaigns and events can also deepen students' understanding of the ethical considerations involved in AI adoption. By bringing in voices from outside the legal academy, institutions can expose students to diverse perspectives on AI ethics. These events can cover a wide range of topics, including bias in AI, transparency, data privacy and the broader societal implications of AI use in the legal profession. Fostering open ethical discussions within legal education institutions is essential for creating a culture of awareness, accountability and critical thinking about the implications of AI adoption. By promoting dialogue, institutions not only ensure that students and faculty are actively engaged in understanding the ethical dimensions of AI, but also contribute to the development of future legal professionals who can navigate and address the complex ethical challenges AI presents. Such discussions are crucial for aligning AI technologies with the principles of justice, fairness and equity that underpin legal education.

1.3.1 Creating a Safe and Inclusive Space for Dialogue

Institutions should establish a safe and inclusive environment where students and faculty feel comfortable discussing ethical dilemmas related to AI without fear of judgement or repercussions. A culture of open dialogue encourages participants to express their concerns, share diverse perspectives and critically evaluate the ethical implications of AI technologies. Steps to foster such an environment include encouraging open participation and moderated discussions. Students and faculty from all backgrounds and levels of expertise should be encouraged to participate in these discussions, ensuring that a variety of viewpoints are represented. This helps to surface a wide range of ethical concerns and fosters a deeper understanding of the societal and professional impacts of AI in legal education. Institutions should ensure that discussions are moderated by individuals with expertise in AI ethics or legal education, creating a structured and respectful atmosphere where participants can share

---

3 M. Lim and A. Allan, 'The Use of Scenarios in Legal Education to Develop Futures Thinking and Sustainability Competencies' (2016) 50 *The Law Teacher* 321.

their views and explore ethical questions. Moderators can guide conversations toward constructive, solution-oriented outcomes.

1.3.2 Integration of AI Ethics Into the Curriculum

To fully prepare students for the ethical challenges posed by AI in the legal profession, ethical discussions must be embedded into the core curriculum. Integrating AI ethics into legal education allows students to critically analyse AI technologies from multiple perspectives, including their implications for legal practice, access to justice and societal equity. Specific approaches to curriculum integration include offering dedicated AI ethics courses, incorporating AI ethics into existing courses and presenting ethical case studies. Institutions can introduce standalone courses that focus on the ethical, legal and societal impacts of AI technologies. These courses should cover key topics such as data privacy, algorithmic bias, transparency, accountability and the ethical considerations involved in the use of AI in legal practice. AI ethics discussions can also be embedded into existing courses on legal theory, professional responsibility and technology law. This allows students to examine ethical issues related to AI in the context of broader legal frameworks and doctrines. Presenting students with case studies involving real-world ethical dilemmas related to AI adoption in law can help them apply ethical reasoning to complex, practical scenarios. For example, students might analyse how bias in AI-driven sentencing tools affects marginalised communities or debate the ethical use of predictive AI technologies in criminal justice.

1.3.3 Scenario-Based Learning for Ethical Reasoning

Scenario-based learning is a powerful tool for encouraging students to engage in ethical reasoning and critically evaluate the implications of AI technologies in dynamic, real-world contexts. By simulating situations where AI might be applied in legal practice, students are prompted to think about the potential legal, ethical and societal consequences of AI decisions. Specific strategies for using scenario-based learning include simulated ethical dilemmas, ethical debates and collaborative problem-solving. Instructors can present students with hypothetical scenarios that involve the use of AI in legal processes, such as automated contract review or predictive policing. Students must then assess the ethical implications of these technologies, considering factors such as fairness, transparency, accountability and potential harm to individuals or communities. Organising debates where students argue for or against the ethical use of specific AI technologies in legal practice encourages them to consider different viewpoints and develop well-reasoned ethical positions. These debates can be used to explore contentious topics such as the use of AI in criminal sentencing or AI-generated legal advice. Students can work in teams to address ethical dilemmas related to AI adoption in the legal field. Collaborative exercises encourage students to think creatively about how to balance the benefits of AI technologies with the ethical obligations of the legal profession.

1.3.4 Engaging the Broader Legal Education Community

Bringing in external voices and experts is essential for exposing students and faculty to diverse perspectives on AI ethics. Organising seminars, workshops and guest speaker sessions allows the legal education community to engage with thought leaders, legal practitioners, technologists and ethicists who can share valuable insights on the ethical dimensions of AI in law. Specific strategies include expert panels and discussions, workshops on AI ethics and guest speaker series. Hosting panels that feature AI experts, ethicists, legal professionals and academics allows students and faculty to engage with cutting-edge debates on the ethical challenges and opportunities presented by AI. Panel discussions can focus on topics such as algorithmic transparency, bias mitigation and the role of AI in promoting or hindering access to justice. Organising workshops where students and faculty can engage in hands-on learning about AI ethics deepens their understanding of key ethical concerns. These workshops can include activities such as analysing AI technologies for biases, exploring the ethical implications of AI in specific legal contexts or developing ethical frameworks for AI adoption in legal practice. Inviting guest speakers from the technology, legal and ethics fields to share their expertise can inspire students and faculty to think critically about the ethical implications of AI. Speakers can present on topics such as the ethical challenges of AI in law firms, the role of AI in protecting or infringing upon human rights and the global impact of AI regulations.

1.3.5 Raising Awareness and Encouraging Ethical Engagement

In addition to formal educational efforts, institutions should raise awareness about the ethical implications of AI technologies through campaigns and events. These initiatives help create a broader culture of ethical engagement within the legal education community, encouraging students and faculty to continuously reflect on the ethical dimensions of AI. Specific initiatives include ethics campaigns, ethics competitions and ethical AI pledges. Institutions can organise awareness campaigns that highlight the importance of AI ethics in legal education and practice. These campaigns can include posters, videos and online resources that emphasise ethical principles such as transparency, fairness and accountability in AI use. Hosting ethics competitions where students present solutions to ethical challenges related to AI adoption can encourage innovative thinking and deepen their understanding of AI ethics. These competitions might involve students developing ethical frameworks for AI use in legal practice or proposing policy solutions to mitigate biases in AI systems. Institutions can encourage students and faculty to take pledges that commit them to upholding ethical standards in the use of AI technologies. These pledges can serve as a reminder of the institution's commitment to responsible AI use and promote a culture of ethical integrity.

1.3.6 Diverse Perspectives and Global Considerations

To ensure that discussions on AI ethics are inclusive and reflective of global realities, institutions should actively seek diverse perspectives from outside the legal academy. AI adoption and its ethical implications vary across different legal systems, cultures and jurisdictions, making it important for students to understand how AI technologies affect diverse populations and legal frameworks. Strategies for incorporating diverse perspectives include global AI ethics dialogues, cross-disciplinary engagement and ethical frameworks in different legal systems. Institutions can organise dialogues with international scholars, legal professionals and technologists to explore how AI ethics are addressed in different regions and legal systems. These dialogues help students appreciate the global impact of AI technologies and the need for international cooperation in developing ethical AI standards. Involving experts from fields such as computer science, philosophy and social justice in ethical discussions broadens students' understanding of AI's societal impact. Cross-disciplinary engagement encourages students to think beyond the legal implications of AI and consider its broader ethical and societal consequences. Institutions can expose students to how different legal systems and cultural contexts approach AI ethics, helping them appreciate the importance of tailoring AI guidelines and policies to fit specific regional needs and values.

Fostering open ethical discussions on AI within legal education is crucial for preparing future legal professionals to navigate the ethical challenges posed by AI technologies. By creating safe spaces for dialogue, integrating AI ethics into the curriculum, engaging in scenario-based learning and inviting external experts to share diverse perspectives, institutions can promote a culture of ethical awareness, critical thinking and accountability. These efforts will equip students with the ethical reasoning skills needed to ensure that AI technologies are used responsibly and fairly in the legal profession, ultimately contributing to the broader goals of justice and equity in society.

Practical Tips

Ethical considerations and practices not only ensure that AI adoption in legal education is conducted responsibly but also contribute to the sustainability and integrity of AI initiatives. They help create a culture of transparency, accountability and ethical awareness within the institution, ultimately benefiting students and the broader legal community. Institutions should strive to create an ethical AI culture by promoting awareness campaigns about the importance of AI ethics and the potential consequences of unethical AI use; engaging faculty, students and staff in discussions about the role of ethics in AI, ensuring that everyone involved in AI initiatives understands the ethical stakes; and incorporating ethical AI practices into institutional policies, making them a core component of AI adoption and implementation.

While the approach set out in this section in many ways addresses important ethical considerations associated with the adoption of AI in legal education, including privacy, bias mitigation, inclusivity, transparency and ownership rights, it is acknowledged that it has its limitations. Practical recommendations have been discussed for addressing ethical challenges, such as establishing AI ethics committees, developing AI ethics guidelines, fostering open ethical discussions and implementing scenario-based learning. By highlighting the importance of ethical considerations in AI adoption and their relevance to sustainability efforts, this strategy aligns ethical practices with sustainability goals, promoting responsible AI use. However, more specific consideration will be required in relation to the implementation of this strategy, such as how to establish AI ethics committees or integrate scenario-based learning into the curriculum. While establishing AI ethics committees and review boards as oversight mechanisms has been proposed already in this book, there may be potential challenges associated with their implementation, such as resource constraints or conflicting interests. Similarly, while curriculum adjustments to cover AI-related topics and ethical considerations have been suggested, the practicalities of integrating these topics into existing curricula will require careful consideration, as there may be potential constraints in doing so.

While this section has highlighted the importance of ethical considerations in AI adoption and offered practical recommendations, further elaboration and specificity in implementation strategies at the institutional level is necessary to effectively address sustainability ethics in relation to the adoption of AI in legal education. There are several key challenges that might arise in implementing these strategies effectively, including the following.

Establishing and Maintaining AI Ethics Committees and Review Boards

Forming ethics committees with experts in AI, law and ethics can be difficult, particularly in institutions with limited access to AI professionals. The interdisciplinary nature of these committees requires knowledge in various fields, which can be hard to source or sustain. Maintaining these committees over time requires financial and human resources. Smaller institutions

Ethical Considerations in AI Adoption 31

or those with limited budgets may struggle to allocate sufficient resources to form and sustain effective oversight bodies. It may be challenging to define the exact role and scope of these committees, particularly as AI technologies evolve rapidly. Committees may face difficulties in keeping up with emerging AI advancements, making continuous oversight a challenge.

Development and Implementation of AI Ethics Guidelines and Policies

While developing AI ethics guidelines is crucial, creating policies that are flexible enough to adapt to evolving technologies while being specific enough to provide actionable guidance can be difficult. Achieving a balance between general ethical principles and specific policy frameworks might be complex. Institutions may face resistance from stakeholders, such as faculty or administrations who may view the creation of AI ethics guidelines as unnecessary bureaucratic red tape. Ensuring buy-in from all levels of the institution is crucial for the successful implementation of these policies. Even with comprehensive guidelines in place, there may be inconsistencies in how they are applied across different faculties or departments. Ensuring uniform adherence to ethical AI practices across an institution is a key challenge.

Open Ethical Discussions and Curriculum Integration

Faculty and students may resist integrating AI ethics into the curriculum, especially if it requires significant shifts in traditional legal education practices. Faculty may lack familiarity with AI technologies, making it difficult to teach these ethical considerations effectively. Institutions may face time constraints when trying to introduce AI ethics modules or discussions into already packed curricula. Additionally, training faculty to facilitate these discussions requires investment in time and resources. Encouraging students to critically engage with ethical AI discussions may prove difficult, especially if students do not immediately see the relevance of AI ethics to their future legal careers. Institutions may need to work hard to demonstrate the importance of these topics.

Transparency and Data Privacy Concerns

Many AI systems, especially those driven by complex ML algorithms, can be difficult to explain even to experts. Achieving full transparency in AI decision-making may not be feasible, leading to challenges in ensuring that users fully understand the rationale behind AI-driven decisions. Ensuring compliance with data privacy regulations, such as the GDPR, can be technically and administratively complex, especially when using AI systems that collect and process sensitive student information. Ethical and legal obligations can conflict with institutional practices, making it challenging to balance data privacy and the effective use of AI tools.

Bias Mitigation and Fairness

Even with efforts to mitigate bias, AI algorithms are often trained on data that contains historical biases. Identifying and correcting biases in these large datasets can be difficult, and ongoing monitoring is required to prevent unintentional discrimination in AI-driven legal education. Institutions with greater access to resources may be better able to implement bias mitigation techniques, while underfunded institutions could struggle to address fairness issues in their AI systems. This discrepancy may lead to further inequities in AI integration across different legal education institutions. Some biases in AI systems stem from inherent limitations in current AI technologies. Until these technical challenges are fully addressed, bias mitigation will remain an ongoing and difficult process.

Fostering Open Ethical Discussions and Cultural Shifts

Encouraging a culture of ethical AI use can face resistance, especially in institutions where there is a lack of awareness about AI ethics or where there is scepticism about the need for such discussions. Building a culture of openness around AI ethics requires consistent effort and engagement across all stakeholders. Organising regular workshops, seminars and guest lectures demands significant institutional resources and time, which may be difficult to allocate consistently, especially if there are competing priorities within the institution.

Intellectual Property and Ownership Issues

The legal landscape surrounding AI-generated content and IP ownership is still evolving. Navigating this evolving legal framework presents a challenge for institutions, faculty and students alike. Institutions may struggle to establish clear ownership policies that reflect both ethical and legal best practices. Disagreements may arise over ownership of AI-generated research, assessments or content – particularly when multiple stakeholders are involved (e.g., students, faculty and external partners). These disputes could create tensions and ethical dilemmas within institutions.

Maintaining Ethical AI Practices Over Time

AI technologies evolve rapidly, making it challenging to maintain ethical standards over time. Institutions may find it difficult to continuously adapt their ethical frameworks and policies to keep pace with these advancements. Ethical AI practices require ongoing oversight, and this continuous monitoring can place a strain on institutional resources. Developing the capacity for regular assessments, audits and revisions to ethical policies can be resource intensive.

Ethical considerations are at the heart of sustainable AI adoption in legal education. By implementing strategies that promote transparency, fairness, inclusivity and data protection, institutions can ensure that AI technologies are used responsibly and in alignment with ethical principles. These efforts contribute to the long-term sustainability of AI initiatives, fostering a legal education system that values justice, equity and the responsible use of technology. Through the establishment of AI ethics committees, the development of ethical guidelines and the integration of AI ethics into the curriculum, law schools can create a culture of ethical AI use that benefits both students and the broader legal community. The implementation of ethical AI practices in legal education faces numerous challenges, ranging from the technical difficulties of maintaining transparency in AI systems to the institutional resistance to curriculum changes. Ensuring ongoing oversight, mitigating bias, addressing data privacy concerns and fostering a culture of open ethical discussions require concerted effort and resource investment. Institutions must carefully navigate these challenges to build sustainable and ethically sound AI-driven legal education systems.

2 Bias Mitigation and Fairness

The sustainability implications of AI biases in legal education are manifold, affecting both the ethical and environmental dimensions of sustainability. Addressing these biases is essential to promote fairness, inclusion and ethical AI practices. Biases in AI algorithms can lead to unfair and discriminatory outcomes in legal education. This raises ethical concerns, as it can perpetuate inequality and hinder students' opportunities based on characteristics such as race, gender or socioeconomic background.[1] Biased AI may inadvertently disadvantage certain student groups by providing unequal access to resources, opportunities or personalised learning experiences. This challenges the sustainability of an equitable educational environment, since AI biases erode trust in educational institutions and AI technologies. For instance, uncertainty can affect user perceptions and interactions with AI.[2] Institutions that fail to address bias issues risk damaging their reputation and sustainability in the long run, and inefficient allocation of educational resources due to biased AI recommendations can lead to wastage of resources and environmental inefficiency. The integration of AI in legal education also involves discussing the ethical and social responsibilities of legal professionals when using AI tools and addressing AI biases.[3] Addressing AI biases in legal education is a vital step in ensuring the sustainability of educational practices. By promoting fairness, equity and ethical AI use, institutions can foster an inclusive learning environment that benefits all students while upholding their ethical and environmental responsibilities. Lowther and Sellick have explored the integration of sustainability literacy into the legal curriculum and this can include ethical considerations, particularly related to bias, fairness and transparency.[4]

---

1 J. Lambert and M. Stevens, 'ChatGPT and Generative AI Technology: A Mixed Bag of Concerns and New Opportunities' (2023) *Computers in the Schools* 1.
2 S. Pan, J. Cui and Y. Mou, 'Desirable or Distasteful ? Exploring Uncertainty in Human-Chatbot Relationships' (2023) *International Journal of Human – Computer Interaction* 1.
3 D. M. Ong, 'Prospects for Integrating an Environmental Sustainability Perspective within the University Law Curriculum in England' (2016) 50 *The Law Teacher* 276.
4 J. Lowther and J. Sellick, 'Embedding Sustainability Literacy in the Legal Curriculum: Reflections on the Plymouth Model' (2016) 50 *The Law Teacher* 307.

DOI: 10.4324/9781003607397-3

Other strategies to address AI biases in legal education include the following.

2.1 Regular Audits for Bias and Fairness

Frequent and systematic audits of AI algorithms and models should be conducted to detect and rectify biases. This involves analysing historical data and model outputs to identify patterns of bias. Regular audits ensure that AI systems remain fair and unbiased over time. Institutions should ensure that training data used for AI models is diverse and representative. This includes considering factors like race, gender, socioeconomic status and geographic location to minimise bias in the data that could be reflected in AI outcomes. Also, establishing ethics review boards or committees responsible for evaluating the ethical implications of AI implementations in legal education can provide independent oversight and guidance on fairness issues. Conducting regular audits for bias and fairness in AI systems is a crucial step toward ensuring that these technologies operate in a manner that is ethical, transparent and equitable. AI-driven tools used in legal education, whether for grading, assessments or providing legal insights, must be continuously monitored to prevent unintentional biases that can skew results and unfairly affect individuals. Bias in AI can result from several factors, including biased training data, unrepresentative datasets or the misapplication of algorithms, all of which can perpetuate systemic inequalities. By implementing frequent and comprehensive audits, institutions can ensure that AI systems remain fair and unbiased over time, contributing to both educational integrity and broader societal justice.

2.1.1 Establishing Systematic and Frequent Audits

Regular audits of AI systems should be embedded as a key practice in legal education institutions. These audits should be systematic, involving a comprehensive review of AI algorithms, training data and outcomes to detect potential biases. Steps involved in conducting these audits include ongoing monitoring, routine checks and external auditors. Institutions should establish a process for ongoing monitoring of AI algorithms, ensuring that audits are not a one-time event but a continuous process of evaluating fairness and ethical compliance. Routine checks should assess the impact of AI outputs on different demographic groups, looking for patterns where certain groups might be disproportionately advantaged or disadvantaged by AI-generated outcomes. For example, AI tools used in legal education may reflect bias in grading or admissions if not properly audited. In some cases, external auditors with expertise in AI ethics and fairness can be invited to provide an independent review. Having a fresh perspective can help detect biases that internal teams may overlook, adding an extra layer of accountability.

2.1.2 Identifying Bias in Training Data

One of the primary sources of bias in AI systems is the training data on which algorithms are built. If the data used to train AI systems is skewed, is unrepresentative or contains historical biases, the AI models will likely replicate and even amplify those biases. Institutions must therefore ensure that the data used is diverse, balanced and free from systemic prejudice. Key strategies for addressing data bias include diverse and representative data, data preprocessing and historical context consideration. The datasets used to train AI systems should reflect the full diversity of the student population, including variables such as race, gender, socioeconomic status, age and geographic location. This ensures that AI outcomes are fair and relevant to all individuals, rather than disproportionately benefiting one group over others. Before feeding data into AI models, institutions should implement preprocessing techniques that detect and remove potential biases from the training data. Techniques such as rebalancing datasets, oversampling underrepresented groups or normalising data distributions can help minimise the risk of bias creeping into AI systems. It is also crucial to understand the historical context of the data. Legal education institutions should recognise that historical legal decisions, case law or datasets used in the past may contain biases reflective of societal inequalities, and incorporating such data into AI models without proper correction can perpetuate these inequities.

2.1.3 Analysing AI Model Outputs

Once trained, AI models must be audited regularly to ensure that their outputs are fair and unbiased. This involves analysing how the AI makes decisions, what outcomes it produces and whether there are disparities in how different groups are affected by these outcomes. Strategies for auditing AI outputs include outcome disparities, testing for fairness and feedback loops. Audits should focus on identifying disparities in outcomes produced by AI systems, such as unequal performance between different demographic groups. For instance, in legal education, an AI system that disproportionately assigns lower scores to certain groups of students based on race, gender or socioeconomic status must be re-examined. Techniques such as fairness testing or "fairness metrics" should be employed to evaluate AI systems. These metrics can help measure whether the system is treating all demographic groups equally and fairly, and whether it aligns with legal and ethical standards. Institutions should also establish mechanisms for gathering feedback from students and faculty about their experiences with AI-driven tools. This can provide valuable insights into any perceived biases or unfairness, which can then be addressed in future audits.

2.1.4 Bias Mitigation Strategies

Once bias has been identified in AI systems, legal education institutions should work proactively to mitigate it. Bias mitigation strategies aim to correct the issues discovered during audits and ensure that the AI systems produce fair and equitable results moving forward. Key bias mitigation strategies include bias correction in algorithms, rebuilding or retraining models, and human oversight. Institutions can use techniques such as algorithmic adjustments to correct for bias. For example, "adversarial debiasing" techniques can be applied to ensure that the AI model actively works to counteract bias in decision-making. If a model is found to be biased, it may need to be retrained on a more balanced and representative dataset. In cases of significant bias, the model may even need to be rebuilt from scratch using better-curated data. AI should be viewed as a tool to augment human decision-making rather than replacing it entirely. Incorporating human oversight in the decision-making process can serve as a check against any biases the AI may introduce. For example, AI-generated recommendations for student assessments can be reviewed by educators before final decisions are made.

2.1.5 Independent Oversight and Ethical Review

Institutions should establish ethics review boards or committees responsible for evaluating the ethical implications of AI implementations, particularly with respect to fairness and bias. These committees can serve as an independent oversight mechanism to ensure that AI practices align with ethical standards. The roles and responsibilities of these committees might include ethics committees for AI oversight, guidance and recommendations and regular review of AI policies. An ethics committee composed of legal experts, AI specialists, ethicists and educators should be tasked with reviewing AI tools and their potential to introduce bias or unethical outcomes. This committee can evaluate the entire lifecycle of AI systems, from data collection to deployment, ensuring that all processes are transparent and ethical. The committee should provide ongoing guidance and recommendations to ensure that AI practices remain aligned with fairness and bias mitigation principles. They should have the authority to suggest modifications or even the discontinuation of AI systems that pose significant ethical concerns. Institutions should task these committees with regularly reviewing and updating institutional policies on AI use to reflect the latest developments in AI ethics and fairness. As AI technologies evolve, so too must the ethical frameworks that govern them.

2.1.6 Transparency and Accountability

Transparency in the audit process is key to maintaining the trust of students, faculty and stakeholders. Institutions should be open about the steps they are taking to ensure that AI systems remain fair and unbiased. Transparency fosters accountability and demonstrates a commitment to ethical AI use. Specific transparency measures include public reporting and clear guidelines for accountability. Institutions should consider reporting the results of AI audits publicly, highlighting steps taken to address any biases found in the system. This can reassure students and faculty that AI systems are being managed responsibly and ethically. Institutions should also establish clear guidelines for holding individuals or teams accountable if bias is detected in AI systems. This may include sanctions for failure to adhere to ethical standards or requirements for retraining staff involved in AI oversight.

Regular audits for bias and fairness are essential to ensuring that AI systems used in legal education operate in an ethical and just manner. By establishing frequent audits, ensuring the diversity and representativeness of training data, and engaging in bias mitigation strategies, institutions can help prevent AI systems from perpetuating societal inequities. Ethics review boards, transparency and accountability measures further reinforce a culture of fairness and ethical responsibility. Through these actions, legal education institutions can ensure that AI tools contribute positively to both the academic environment and broader societal goals of justice and equity.

2.2 Transparency and Explainability Features

Transparency reports that detail how AI algorithms and models operate should be developed. These reports should include information on data sources, model architectures and decision-making processes. Transparency helps stakeholders understand the system's inner workings. Implementing AI systems with explainability features allows users to comprehend the rationale behind AI-generated recommendations or decisions. Explainability tools facilitate transparency and help identify potential sources of bias, so AI tools designed to audit for bias in algorithms should be leveraged. These tools can detect and flag potential bias in model outputs automatically, making it easier to identify and address fairness issues. Transparency and explainability are foundational principles in the ethical and responsible use of AI, particularly in high-stakes environments like legal education. Transparency ensures that stakeholders understand how AI systems work, fostering trust, accountability and informed decision-making. Explainability, on the other hand, allows users to comprehend how AI systems arrive at specific conclusions or recommendations, thereby demystifying the often complex and opaque decision-making processes that AI models employ. Together, these features not only help to build confidence in AI systems but also allow for the identification and rectification of biases and other ethical concerns, ensuring that AI is used fairly and responsibly.

2.2.1 Developing Transparency Reports

One of the most effective ways to ensure transparency in AI systems is through the creation of detailed transparency reports. These reports should offer comprehensive insights into how AI models are developed, trained and deployed, allowing stakeholders – including students, educators and administrators – to gain a deeper understanding of the system's inner workings. Key elements that should be included in transparency reports are data sources, model architectures, decision-making processes and model updates and changes. Transparency reports should identify the sources of data used to train AI models clearly. This includes information about the dataset's origins, representativeness and any preprocessing steps applied to the data. Knowing the data sources helps users assess the potential for bias or limitations in the AI's outputs. The underlying architecture of AI models – such as whether they use ML, deep learning or neural networks – should be explained in understandable terms. While not every stakeholder needs to grasp technical specifics, providing a high-level overview of how the model operates can build trust in the system. Transparency reports should also outline the decision-making processes of AI systems. For instance, if an AI system is used for grading or legal research, the report should explain how the AI arrives at its conclusions or recommendations. This could include detailing which features or variables the AI considers most important when making decisions and how it weighs different inputs. AI systems evolve over time as they are retrained or fine-tuned to improve performance. Transparency reports should document any updates to the model, including changes to the algorithm, data sources or decision-making processes. This ongoing documentation ensures that stakeholders are aware of the evolution of AI systems and any new ethical or fairness implications that may arise from changes.

2.2.2 Implementing Explainability Features

AI systems should be designed with robust explainability features that allow users to easily understand how the model arrived at a particular output. Explainability is especially important in legal education, where AI systems may be used for tasks like evaluating student performance, providing legal research insights or assisting with case analysis. Explainability tools should provide user-friendly explanations, feature importance and interactive explanations. AI systems should be equipped with interfaces that offer clear and comprehensible explanations of how decisions or recommendations are made. For instance, if an AI tool is used to grade assignments, it should be able to explain why a particular grade was assigned, highlighting the key factors that contributed to the decision. Explainability features should show users which factors or variables were most important in the AI's decision-making process. For example, in legal research tools, the system could display which legal precedents or statutes were most influential in generating a recommendation, enabling students or faculty to verify the appropriateness of the AI's conclusions. Advanced explainability tools could allow users to interact with the model to test different inputs and see how the AI's recommendations change. This can provide deeper insights into how the AI system operates and whether its decision-making processes are fair and reliable.

2.2.3 Leveraging AI Tools for Bias Auditing

AI systems designed to audit other AI algorithms for bias play a crucial role in maintaining fairness and accountability. These auditing tools can detect and flag potential sources of bias automatically, making it easier for institutions to address fairness concerns. Such tools can help institutions to monitor bias continuously, flagging model outputs and highlighting data disparities. Bias auditing tools can be set up to continuously monitor AI systems for signs of bias in real time. By flagging potential issues as they arise, institutions can intervene and make adjustments before biased outputs affect students or decision-making processes. Bias detection tools can flag AI-generated outputs that may reflect unfair or biased outcomes. For instance, if an AI system tends to favour certain demographic groups in admissions decisions or performance assessments, these tools can alert administrators to potential fairness issues automatically. Bias auditing tools can also help institutions detect disparities in the data used to train AI models. These tools can identify whether certain groups are underrepresented in the training data, potentially leading to biased outcomes. Once these disparities are detected, institutions can take steps to re-balance the dataset or apply bias mitigation techniques to ensure fairer outcomes.

2.2.4 Detecting and Addressing Fairness Issues

Transparency and explainability features also play a critical role in identifying and addressing fairness issues in AI systems. By making AI systems more transparent and understandable, institutions can detect and resolve potential biases or fairness concerns. Some key strategies for using these features to promote fairness include ethical oversight committees, user feedback mechanisms, retraining and adjustment. Transparency and explainability tools can provide valuable information to ethical oversight committees which are tasked with reviewing AI systems for fairness and ethical compliance. These committees can use the insights provided by explainability tools to make informed decisions about whether the AI system is operating fairly and in accordance with ethical guidelines. Institutions should establish feedback mechanisms that allow students, faculty and other stakeholders to report any concerns they have about the fairness or transparency of AI systems. By incorporating feedback into regular audits and reviews, institutions can ensure that AI systems are improving and aligning with ethical standards continuously. When fairness issues are detected, institutions can retrain AI models on more diverse and representative datasets or adjust the algorithms to correct for biases. Explainability features help identify the specific areas where these adjustments need to be made, allowing for more targeted interventions.

2.2.5 Building Stakeholder Trust and Engagement

Implementing transparency and explainability features in AI systems helps build trust among students, educators and other stakeholders in the institution. When users understand how AI systems work and have the ability to scrutinise the decision-making process, they are more likely to engage with the technology in a positive and informed manner. Key benefits of fostering trust through transparency and explainability include increased user confidence, encouraging ethical behaviour and promoting informed AI adoption. When users have clear insights into how AI systems operate, they are more likely to trust the results and recommendations generated by these systems. This confidence is especially important in educational contexts, where students and faculty rely on AI for critical tasks like grading, research and legal analysis. Transparency and explainability features promote ethical behaviour within institutions by encouraging accountability. When AI systems are transparent, stakeholders can hold institutions responsible for the ethical use of AI, ensuring that biases or unethical practices are addressed promptly. Explainability tools allow users to better understand the benefits and limitations of AI systems, empowering them to use AI in a more informed and responsible manner. By making AI systems transparent, institutions can promote the responsible adoption of AI in legal education and ensure that users are aware of potential biases or limitations.

Incorporating transparency and explainability features into AI systems used in legal education is essential for fostering trust, ensuring fairness and promoting accountability. Transparency reports provide stakeholders with detailed insights into how AI models operate, while explainability tools allow users to understand the rationale behind AI-generated decisions. Leveraging bias auditing tools and fostering continuous monitoring helps institutions detect and address fairness issues before they negatively affect students or decision-making processes. Ultimately, transparency and explainability features play a crucial role in ensuring that AI systems are used ethically, responsibly and equitably, aligning with the values and goals of legal education institutions.

2.3 Research and Development of Bias Mitigation Techniques

Institutions should encourage interdisciplinary research collaborations between computer scientists, legal experts, ethicists and social scientists.

Such collaborations can lead to innovative bias mitigation techniques and tools. Investing in research and development efforts focused on creating bias-resistant AI algorithms can mitigate bias during data processing and model training. Standardised fairness benchmarks and evaluation metrics specific to legal education should be developed to serve as objective criteria for assessing the fairness of AI systems. Training programmes and workshops should be provided for data scientists and AI developers on bias mitigation techniques and best practices to educate them on the potential sources of bias in legal data and how to address them. Engaging with the legal education community, including students, faculty and practitioners, can gather input on fairness concerns and solicit feedback on AI systems' impact on diverse groups. Implementing bias auditing frameworks that enable continuous monitoring and assessment of AI systems for fairness can identify and rectify biases as they emerge. In order to ensure that AI systems used in legal education are fair and equitable, institutions must prioritise the research and development of advanced bias mitigation techniques. Bias in AI systems, often stemming from historical data or algorithmic design, can perpetuate inequalities and negatively affect the fairness of outcomes. By fostering interdisciplinary research, investing in bias-resistant technologies and developing fairness benchmarks, legal education institutions can create AI systems that not only comply with ethical standards but also reflect the values of fairness and inclusivity essential to the legal profession.

2.3.1 Interdisciplinary Research Collaborations

Encouraging interdisciplinary research collaborations is essential to addressing the complex challenge of AI bias. Legal education institutions should foster partnerships between experts from different fields, including computer scientists (specialists in AI and machine learning who understand how algorithms are designed and trained); legal experts (professionals who can provide insights into the legal implications of AI use, including fairness and equity within the legal context); ethicists (scholars who explore the moral and ethical dimensions of AI technologies, particularly the societal impact of biased AI systems); and social scientists (experts who can analyse how AI bias affects different demographic groups and societal structures, helping to shape more equitable AI systems). These collaborations are crucial in developing innovative approaches to bias mitigation. For example, legal experts may help computer scientists understand how AI bias could lead to discrimination in legal decision-making, while social scientists may contribute to identifying underrepresented groups in the training data. Together, they can design AI models that are more sensitive to these issues, creating systems that are more fair and more aligned with ethical principles.

2.3.2 Investing in Bias-Resistant AI Algorithms

Developing bias-resistant AI algorithms is one of the most important steps in mitigating bias in legal education. Institutions should invest in research and development efforts that focus on creating algorithms that can detect and mitigate bias at various stages of the AI process, including data collection, model training and post-processing. AI systems are often trained on historical data, which may reflect existing biases. Institutions should focus on developing methods for identifying and correcting biased data before it is used to train AI models. This could include techniques for balancing underrepresented groups in datasets or methods for removing biased features that could lead to unfair outcomes. Bias can be introduced during the model training phase if the algorithms inadvertently learn and reinforce biased patterns from the data. Developing bias-resistant algorithms that can detect these patterns and adjust for them in real time is critical. For instance, some ML techniques use fairness constraints that penalise models for biased behaviour, helping to ensure that the AI system produces fairer outcomes. After an AI model is deployed, bias mitigation techniques should be used to ensure that the outputs remain fair. Post-processing techniques can adjust biased predictions or recommendations made by the AI system, ensuring that they do not disadvantage certain groups unfairly. Investing in these advanced bias mitigation methods can help institutions create AI systems that are less likely to perpetuate discrimination or unfairness in legal education and practice.

2.3.3 Developing Fairness Benchmarks and Evaluation Metrics

To assess the fairness of AI systems in legal education, it is important to establish standardised fairness benchmarks and evaluation metrics. These criteria can serve as objective tools for evaluating whether an AI system is operating in a fair and unbiased manner. Specifically, institutions should create legal education-specific fairness metrics, establish benchmarks for AI systems and update fairness standards regularly. Fairness metrics tailored to the unique context of legal education are crucial. For example, evaluation metrics could focus on ensuring that AI-generated legal research does not favour precedents that reflect historical biases disproportionately, or on ensuring that AI-assisted grading tools evaluate students equitably, regardless of background or identity. Creating benchmarks for AI systems allows institutions to compare the performance of different algorithms in terms of fairness and bias mitigation. For instance, benchmarks could assess how well AI systems predict legal case outcomes without introducing bias or how fairly they allocate educational resources among students. As AI systems evolve, so too should the fairness benchmarks used to evaluate them. Legal education institutions must continuously update these standards to reflect advances in AI technology and changing societal expectations of fairness and equity. By establishing clear and measurable criteria for evaluating fairness, institutions can assess and improve the ethical performance of their AI systems more effectively.

2.3.4 Training Programmes and Workshops for Bias Mitigation

Training and education are key to ensuring that those who design and develop AI systems are aware of the potential sources of bias and are equipped with the tools to address them. Legal education institutions should offer dedicated training programmes and workshops for data scientists and AI developers. Data scientists working on AI systems must understand the potential biases inherent in legal data, as well as how to apply bias mitigation techniques during model development. Workshops could cover topics such as the ethical implications of biased datasets, how to detect and eliminate biases during model training and best practices for ensuring that AI systems produce fair outcomes. AI developers should be trained in the latest bias mitigation methods and tools. These workshops could introduce developers to new algorithms and techniques designed to minimise bias – such as fairness constraints, adversarial debiasing and re-weighting data – to ensure balanced representation. By educating the people responsible for designing and building AI systems, institutions can ensure that bias mitigation is a core consideration throughout the AI development process.

2.3.5 Engaging With the Legal Education Community

Gathering input from the broader legal education community – including students, faculty and practitioners – is essential for identifying fairness concerns and ensuring that AI systems reflect the values of diversity and inclusion. Institutions should solicit feedback on AI systems, conduct surveys and focus groups, and collaborate with legal practitioners. Regular feedback from students, faculty and legal professionals can help identify areas where AI systems may be falling short in terms of fairness. For example, students may point out instances where AI-based assessments are biased or discriminatory, allowing institutions to address these issues promptly. Institutions can organise surveys and focus groups to better understand the impact of AI systems on diverse groups within the legal education community. This feedback can inform future AI development efforts and help shape policies and practices that promote fairness. Engaging with legal practitioners can provide valuable insights into how AI systems operate in real-world legal settings. Practitioners can offer feedback on the fairness and inclusivity of AI tools, which can be used to refine and improve AI systems used in legal education. By involving the community in the development and evaluation of AI systems, institutions can ensure that their AI tools are equitable and meet the needs of all users.

2.3.6 Implementing Bias Auditing Frameworks

Institutions should implement bias auditing frameworks that enable continuous monitoring of AI systems for fairness and bias. These frameworks allow for ongoing assessments of AI systems as they evolve, ensuring that fairness issues are detected and addressed in a timely manner. Key elements of a bias auditing framework include automated bias detection tools, regular audits of AI models and corrective actions. Bias auditing frameworks should incorporate automated tools that continuously monitor AI systems for biased behaviour. These tools can flag instances of unfair outcomes, allowing institutions to intervene and correct the bias. Institutions should conduct regular audits of their AI models to ensure that they remain fair and unbiased over time. These audits could involve reviewing model outputs, checking for disparities in how different demographic groups are treated and assessing the overall fairness of the system. When biases are detected, institutions should have a clear process for addressing these issues. Corrective actions could include retraining AI models on more representative datasets, adjusting algorithms to account for fairness constraints or modifying the system to eliminate biased behaviour. By implementing these auditing frameworks, institutions can ensure that their AI systems remain fair, transparent and aligned with ethical principles over time.

The research and development of bias mitigation techniques are essential for ensuring that AI systems used in legal education operate in a fair and equitable manner. By fostering interdisciplinary collaborations, investing in bias-resistant algorithms and developing standardised fairness benchmarks, institutions can create AI systems that reflect the ethical values of fairness and inclusivity. Engaging with the legal education community and implementing bias auditing frameworks ensures that these systems remain accountable, transparent and continuously improving. Through these efforts, legal education institutions can harness the power of AI while safeguarding against the risks of bias and discrimination.

Practical Tips

Incorporating bias mitigation strategies into AI-driven legal education ensures that AI systems not only enhance efficiency but also uphold principles of fairness and equity. By proactively addressing bias and promoting transparency and research, institutions can create a more inclusive and responsible learning environment that benefits all students and stakeholders. The strategy set out in this chapter addresses various aspects of bias mitigation and fairness in AI adoption, including ethical considerations, environmental implications and social responsibilities of legal professionals. By highlighting the importance of addressing biases to promote fairness and inclusion in legal education, this approach underscores the ethical imperative of mitigating AI biases. Practical recommendations have been put forward for addressing AI biases in legal education – such as regular audits, transparency features and the research and development of bias mitigation techniques – providing actionable steps for institutions to implement. However, there may be potential challenges in implementing these recommendations. While various strategies for addressing AI biases have been discussed, institutions may also encounter potential challenges or barriers in implementing these strategies, such as resource constraints and technological limitations, that will need to be negotiated carefully. Ultimately, while the importance of bias mitigation and fairness in AI adoption in legal education should not be understated, the success of the practical recommendations considered in this section in order to address sustainability ethics in relation to the adoption of AI very much depends on overcoming the challenges of implementing these proposals.

The challenges associated with bias mitigation and fairness in AI-driven legal education are numerous and complex. Addressing these challenges requires careful planning, collaboration and continuous effort. Some key challenges are described in what follows.

Detecting and Quantifying Bias

Identifying bias in AI algorithms can be difficult, especially when biases are subtle or hidden within large datasets. Bias can emerge from the training data, model design or deployment practices, and understanding where it originates is not always straightforward. Failure to detect bias accurately can perpetuate discrimination and lead to unfair educational outcomes. Legal education institutions risk embedding these biases into the learning process, which affects the overall fairness and inclusivity of their programmes. Regular audits and transparency efforts are essential, but conducting these processes thoroughly requires significant resources, including skilled personnel and technological tools for auditing AI systems.

Bias in Training Data

AI models learn from data, and if the training data used to develop the model is biased, the model itself will reflect those biases. Legal education data can be particularly prone to bias, especially if it includes historical inequalities or systemic discrimination patterns. Using biased data for training AI can lead to inequitable recommendations, resource allocation and assessment methods. For example, certain student groups may receive less favourable results or opportunities, perpetuating inequality. Ensuring diversity and fairness in training data is a significant challenge. Collecting and curating large, representative datasets requires considerable time and resources – and even then, it may not eliminate bias entirely.

Transparency and Explainability

While transparency and explainability are crucial for addressing bias, making complex AI systems fully transparent can be difficult. The inner workings of AI algorithms, especially ML models, are often opaque – even to experts. Without explainability, students, faculty and administrators may not fully understand how AI systems make decisions. This can reduce trust in AI technologies and make it difficult to identify and address biases. Developing explainability tools for AI systems is technically challenging, especially for advanced models like neural networks, which operate as "black boxes." Achieving a balance between transparency and performance is difficult and may require significant investment in research and development.

Continuous Monitoring and Auditing

AI models evolve over time, and biases can emerge as systems are used in real-world settings. Continuous monitoring and auditing are necessary to ensure that fairness is maintained throughout the lifecycle of AI systems. Failure to audit AI systems continuously can lead to biases being introduced or exacerbated as new data is processed or models are updated. Legal education institutions may find that their AI systems drift from their original fairness goals. Regular audits require sustained funding, technical expertise and the involvement of multiple stakeholders, including ethics boards. Maintaining long-term monitoring efforts can be resource intensive and may be difficult to justify in the face of competing institutional priorities.

Cost and Resource Constraints

Bias mitigation strategies – such as regular audits, explainability tools and training for developers – require significant financial and human resources. Many legal education institutions may face budgetary constraints that limit their ability to fully address bias issues. Resource constraints may force institutions to prioritise other aspects of AI integration, leaving bias mitigation underfunded or underdeveloped. This can result in inequitable AI systems that perpetuate bias and unfair outcomes. Securing funding and resources for bias mitigation is challenging, particularly in educational settings where budgets are already stretched. Legal education institutions may need to make difficult trade-offs between technological innovation and ethical considerations.

Ethical and Legal Complexities

Addressing bias in AI systems also involves navigating complex ethical and legal issues. AI systems used in legal education must comply with data protection laws, such as GDPR, and adhere to ethical standards related to fairness, privacy and transparency. Failing to navigate these complexities can expose institutions to legal liabilities and ethical criticism. Institutions must ensure that AI systems comply with evolving legal and ethical standards, which can be challenging to implement in a dynamic and rapidly changing field like AI. Keeping up with changes in legal and ethical frameworks requires ongoing legal expertise and interdisciplinary collaboration. This adds another layer of complexity to the already difficult task of bias mitigation.

Resistance to Change

There may be resistance from faculty, staff or students to adopting bias mitigation techniques, especially if it requires changes to existing systems or workflows. Some stakeholders may view AI tools as neutral or objective and may not see the need for extensive bias mitigation efforts. Without buy-in from all stakeholders, the implementation of bias mitigation strategies can be slow or ineffective. Resistance to change can hinder the institution's ability to create a fair and equitable learning environment. Changing mindsets and fostering a culture of fairness and transparency requires effective communication, education and leadership. This is often a slow process, and achieving full consensus can be difficult.

Developing Bias-Resistant Algorithms

Research into bias-resistant algorithms is still in its early stages, and developing AI systems that are truly immune to bias is an ongoing challenge. Even with the best efforts, bias can still emerge from unforeseen sources, such as unintended correlations in data. AI systems in legal education may continue to exhibit bias despite attempts to eliminate it, potentially leading to unfair outcomes for students and faculty. Creating bias-resistant algorithms requires significant research and interdisciplinary collaboration, involving not just data scientists but also ethicists, legal professionals and educators. This kind of collaboration is resource intensive and may take years to yield results.

Mitigating bias and ensuring fairness in AI-driven legal education presents several significant challenges, including technical complexities, resource constraints, legal and ethical issues, and the need for continuous monitoring. Addressing these challenges requires a proactive, collaborative and sustained effort from institutions, with a strong focus on interdisciplinary research, transparency and ethical AI practices. While the path forward may be difficult, navigating these challenges successfully is critical to creating an equitable and sustainable AI ecosystem in legal education. Incorporating bias mitigation strategies into AI-driven legal education is essential for ensuring that AI systems enhance efficiency without compromising fairness or equity. By promoting transparency, conducting regular audits and investing in research, legal education institutions can create a more inclusive learning environment that benefits all students and stakeholders. These efforts also contribute to the long-term sustainability of AI adoption, ensuring that ethical principles are upheld as technology continues to evolve. Institutions that prioritise bias mitigation will foster trust, promote fairness and contribute to the broader goals of ethical AI integration in education.

3 Digital Divide Mitigation

The digital divide is a pressing concern in the context of AI adoption in legal education, representing a significant sustainability challenge. It pertains to the gap in access to digital technologies and the internet, and how this divide can further widen disparities in educational opportunities and outcomes. When addressing the sustainability challenges of AI in legal education, it is essential to consider how the broader digital transformation affects the integration of AI tools and resources.[1] This concern reflects broader discussions about the digital transformation of education. Digital inclusion plays a pivotal role in the overall sustainability of AI adoption in legal education. It ensures that AI-driven educational resources are accessible to all students, regardless of their socioeconomic status or geographical location. This promotes educational equity, addressing disparities in access and opportunity. Bullows emphasises the importance of preparing students with the digital skills needed to navigate AI-driven legal research tools sustainably.[2] When students from diverse backgrounds and abilities can fully engage with AI-powered tools and online content, it creates a more inclusive learning environment. Inclusivity fosters a sense of belonging and supports diverse learning needs.[3] Adaptive learning approaches can also help address diverse student needs and promote long-term sustainability by improving learning outcomes.[4] Institutions invest significant resources in AI adoption; digital inclusion maximises the return on these investments by ensuring that a broader range of students can benefit from AI-powered educational tools, reducing the risk of resource wastage. Promoting digital inclusion aligns with sustainability goals by reducing

---

1 M. Smith, 'Integrating Technology in Contemporary Legal Education' (2020) 54 *The Law Teacher* 209.
2 A. Bullows, 'How Technology is Changing the Legal Sector' (2021) 55 *The Law Teacher* 258.
3 A. R. Ellis and E. Slade, 'A New Era of Learning: Considerations for ChatGPT as a Tool to Enhance Statistics and Data Science Education' (2023) *Journal of Statistics and Data Science Education* 1.
4 S. Hopcan and colleagues, 'Artificial Intelligence in Special Education: A Systematic Review' (2022) *Interactive Learning Environments* 1.

the environmental impact of education: when students can access resources online, there is a reduced need for physical materials, leading to resource conservation.

To mitigate the digital divide in AI-driven legal education and sustain digital inclusion initiatives over time, institutions can implement the following measures.

3.1 Provide Subsidies and Scholarships

Offering financial subsidies or scholarships to students who lack access to essential digital devices and internet connectivity can help bridge the affordability gap, making technology more accessible. Establishing device-lending programmes that provide students with laptops or tablets on a loan basis allows them to access online resources and engage in AI-driven education without the burden of purchasing costly devices. Institutions should collaborate with internet service providers (ISPs) to offer discounted or subsidised internet plans to students in need and ensure that these plans meet the bandwidth requirements for online learning. Access to digital tools and reliable internet connectivity is critical for students to fully participate in AI-driven education, particularly in legal education where emerging technologies are increasingly integrated into the learning process. However, many students, particularly those from low-income or underserved communities, may struggle to afford the necessary devices or internet services. To address this digital divide, institutions can implement targeted financial assistance programmes, such as subsidies and scholarships, as well as collaborate with service providers to offer affordable solutions. These efforts can ensure that all students, regardless of their financial circumstances, have equitable access to educational technologies.

3.1.1 *Financial Subsidies and Scholarships for Digital Devices*

Offering financial subsidies or scholarships can reduce significantly the financial burden on students who cannot afford the essential digital devices needed for AI-driven learning. To do this, institutions should establish targeted scholarship programmes, provide technology vouchers and expand existing financial aid programmes. Institutions can create dedicated scholarship programmes aimed at helping students who lack the financial means to purchase laptops, tablets or other digital tools. These scholarships could be need-based, prioritising students from economically disadvantaged backgrounds, and could cover a portion or the full cost of purchasing necessary devices. In addition to scholarships, universities can offer technology vouchers that allow students to buy devices at reduced prices. These vouchers could be redeemed through partnerships with tech companies, which could provide special discounts for students in need. This programme could be especially helpful for students who are unable to receive a full scholarship but still require financial assistance to access the technology necessary for their education. Universities can also expand their existing financial aid programmes to include a specific allocation for purchasing digital devices. This could be built into tuition assistance packages, making it easier for students to receive the necessary tools for AI-based learning without incurring additional costs.

3.1.2 Device-Lending Programmes

In addition to providing financial assistance, institutions can establish device-lending programmes that offer students access to laptops, tablets or other necessary digital tools on a temporary or loan basis. Key strategies include creating digital device libraries, prioritising underserved students and offering flexible loan terms. Universities can set up device-lending libraries that allow students to borrow laptops, tablets or other digital tools for the duration of a semester or academic year. This provides a practical and cost-effective way for students to access the technology they need without the burden of purchasing expensive devices. Device-lending programmes should prioritise students from low-income backgrounds or those living in areas with limited access to technology. By focusing on these students, institutions can ensure that those most in need benefit from these resources. Universities should ensure that device-lending programmes are flexible and responsive to students' needs. For example, students may need to borrow devices for extended periods, particularly if they face long-term financial constraints. Offering flexible loan terms ensures that students have continuous access to technology throughout their studies.

3.1.3 Collaboration With Internet Service Providers

For many students, the lack of reliable and high-speed internet connectivity is a significant barrier to accessing AI-driven education. Universities should collaborate with ISPs to address this issue by offering discounted or subsidised internet plans. Potential strategies include negotiating discounted internet plans, subsidising internet costs for students and ensuring minimum bandwidth requirements. Institutions can collaborate with ISPs to negotiate special discounted internet plans for students. These plans could offer affordable rates for students who qualify based on financial need, ensuring that they receive adequate bandwidth to access online learning resources and participate in virtual classes. In some cases, institutions could go a step further by directly subsidising students' internet costs, particularly for those in rural or underserved areas where access to reliable internet is limited. Subsidising these costs can help ensure that students can fully participate in AI-enhanced learning activities, regardless of their geographical location. When negotiating internet plans, universities should work with ISPs to ensure that the bandwidth offered is sufficient to meet the requirements for AI-driven online learning, such as accessing high-quality video lectures, real-time collaboration tools and AI-powered educational platforms.

3.1.4 Expanding Access to On-Campus Resources

For students who are unable to secure home access to devices or the internet, institutions should also expand access to on-campus resources. This can include creating more accessible computer labs and offering on-campus Wi-Fi access. Universities can ensure that on-campus computer labs are well equipped with up-to-date devices and software that students need to engage in AI-driven learning. Additionally, institutions should extend the operating hours of these labs to provide students with more opportunities to use them outside of standard class times. Providing free and reliable on-campus Wi-Fi in common areas, libraries and student dormitories can be a crucial resource for students who cannot afford internet access at home. This gives students the ability to access online resources while on campus.

Providing subsidies, scholarships and access to affordable internet connectivity are essential strategies for ensuring equitable access to AI-driven legal education. By offering financial support, creating device-lending programmes and collaborating with ISPs, institutions can help bridge the digital divide and enable all students to benefit from emerging technologies, regardless of their financial circumstances. These measures not only improve access to AI-enhanced learning but also contribute to creating a more inclusive and equitable educational environment.

3.2 Accessibility for Individuals With Disabilities

All online learning platforms and AI tools used in legal education should adhere to accessibility standards such as Web Content Accessibility Guidelines (WCAG).[5] This includes providing alternative formats, screen reader compatibility and keyboard navigation. Promoting the use of assistive technologies – such as screen readers, voice recognition software and text-to-speech tools – supports students with disabilities in accessing AI-driven resources. Faculty should be encouraged to design inclusive course materials and use AI tools that are accessible to individuals with disabilities. Ensuring that all students, including those with disabilities, can access and benefit from AI-driven

---

5 World Wide Web Consortium (W3C), 'Web Content Accessibility Guidelines (WCAG) 2.1' (2018) <www.w3.org/TR/WCAG21/>.

legal education is essential for creating an inclusive and equitable learning environment. Institutions must be proactive in adopting accessibility standards and assistive technologies to support students with varying abilities. As AI tools and online learning platforms become integral to legal education, it is crucial that they are designed and implemented in a way that is fully accessible to individuals with disabilities. This includes compliance with widely recognised accessibility guidelines, the promotion of assistive technologies and the creation of inclusive course materials.

3.2.1 Adherence to Accessibility Standards

All online learning platforms, AI tools and educational resources should comply with recognised accessibility standards such as the WCAG, which set benchmarks for ensuring digital content is accessible to people with disabilities, including those with visual, auditory, physical, speech, cognitive and neurological impairments. To adhere to these standards, institutions should provide alternative formats, ensure screen reader compatibility and implement keyboard navigation. Ensure that all online content, including AI-generated resources, is available in multiple formats. For example, offering lecture transcripts alongside video or audio content enables students with hearing impairments to engage with materials effectively. Platforms and tools should be fully compatible with screen readers, which assist visually impaired students by reading text aloud. Institutions should regularly test AI tools and online platforms to ensure that they work seamlessly with screen readers, including AI-generated text and legal research tools. Many individuals with physical disabilities rely on keyboard navigation instead of a mouse. Ensuring that AI platforms and online learning tools are fully navigable via keyboard shortcuts is critical for students with motor impairments. This includes making sure that interactive elements such as forms, buttons and menus are accessible through keyboard commands.

3.2.2 Promotion and Integration of Assistive Technologies

AI-driven education platforms must promote and integrate assistive technologies to support students with disabilities. These technologies can greatly enhance the learning experience for students with specific needs and empower them to engage fully with AI tools and content. Key assistive technologies include screen readers, voice recognition software, text-to-speech tools and speech-to-text tools. As mentioned, screen readers are essential for visually impaired students to access text-based content. Institutions should ensure that all legal databases, research tools and AI-generated legal analyses are fully compatible with screen readers. Students with physical disabilities that limit their ability to type or use a mouse may rely on voice recognition software. Legal education platforms should support this technology by allowing students to navigate and interact with AI tools using voice commands. Text-to-speech software is helpful for students with learning disabilities, such as dyslexia or those who find it easier to process information by listening. AI tools that automatically convert legal texts or research findings into speech can make complex materials more accessible to a broader range of learners. For students with physical or learning disabilities that affect their ability to write, speech-to-text tools are crucial. These tools allow students to dictate responses, legal analyses or even exam answers, which the system then converts into written text.

3.2.3 *Inclusive Course Design*

Faculty play a critical role in ensuring that course materials are designed with accessibility in mind. As AI tools become more integrated into legal education, instructors should be trained to design course content that accommodates students with disabilities. Strategies to promote inclusive course design include designing for universal access, accessible AI-enhanced materials and providing alternative assessments. Faculty should follow the principles of Universal Design for Learning (UDL; see Section 3.3.5), which encourages the creation of flexible learning environments that accommodate diverse student needs. This involves offering multiple means of engagement, representation and expression, ensuring that all students can access and demonstrate their understanding of the material. Instructors should ensure that AI-powered tools and resources, such as automated legal research platforms or AI-based case analysis tools, are accessible to all students. This could involve collaborating with the developers of AI systems to ensure that they meet accessibility standards. Students with disabilities may face challenges with traditional assessments or AI-driven evaluations. Instructors should offer alternative assessment methods – such as oral presentations, take-home exams or project-based assessments – to ensure that students with disabilities can demonstrate their knowledge and skills in ways that suit their abilities.

3.2.4 *Continuous Monitoring and Feedback*

Ensuring accessibility is not a one-time task but requires ongoing monitoring and improvement. Institutions must establish mechanisms to regularly assess the accessibility of AI tools and online platforms, making adjustments based on student feedback. Strategies include regular accessibility audits, collection of student feedback and responsive support systems. Law schools can conduct periodic audits of AI systems, legal databases and learning platforms to ensure that they comply with evolving accessibility standards. These audits should include input from accessibility experts, as well as students who rely on assistive technologies. Institutions should actively seek feedback from students with disabilities about their experiences using AI-driven tools and online resources. Regular surveys, focus groups and feedback forms can provide valuable insights into the accessibility of digital platforms and highlight areas for improvement. Law schools can stablish dedicated support services for students with disabilities who encounter challenges in accessing AI tools or learning platforms. These services should offer technical assistance, troubleshooting and personalised support to ensure that all students can fully engage with the educational content.

3.2.5 Faculty and Staff Training

In addition to designing inclusive course materials, faculty and staff should receive regular training on accessibility best practices and assistive technologies. This ensures that they are equipped to support students with disabilities effectively. Training should cover awareness of disabilities and accessibility needs, use of assistive technologies and creating accessible content. Faculty should be aware of the diverse needs of students with disabilities and how AI tools and platforms may present unique challenges for these students. Understanding the range of disabilities and how they affect learning is essential for creating an inclusive environment. Faculty should be familiar with the assistive technologies available to students and how they integrate with AI-driven legal education tools. They should also know how to support students in using these technologies effectively. Faculty should be trained to create digital content – such as lecture slides, portable document format (PDF) files and videos – which adhere to accessibility standards. This includes using accessible file formats, providing alternate text for images and offering transcripts for audio or video materials.

Ensuring accessibility for individuals with disabilities in AI-driven legal education is essential for promoting inclusivity and equity. By adhering to accessibility standards, integrating assistive technologies and designing inclusive course materials, institutions can create a learning environment that supports all students. Ongoing monitoring, feedback collection and faculty training are critical to maintaining and improving accessibility as AI tools continue to evolve. Institutions that prioritise accessibility not only comply with legal and ethical obligations but also foster a more diverse and inclusive educational experience for all learners.

3.3 Digital Inclusion Initiatives

Digital literacy programmes, which equip students with the skills needed to navigate online learning environments and utilise AI tools effectively, can be integrated into the curriculum. Smith also highlights the importance of educators adapting to technological advancements.[6] Collaborating with local organisations, libraries and community centres, and providing access to technology and training in underserved communities, extends digital inclusion efforts beyond the campus. Establishing programmes for recycling, donating used devices to students in need and encouraging the recycling of outdated technology reduces electronic waste (e-waste) while promoting digital inclusion. Institutions should embrace the principles of UDL, which emphasise flexible teaching methods that accommodate diverse learning needs, including those related to digital access. Collecting feedback from students regarding their digital access challenges and experiences can be used to refine and expand digital inclusion initiatives. Raising awareness about the digital divide and the importance of digital inclusion within the legal education community and engaging students, faculty and staff in discussions helps to address disparities in access. Continuously monitoring data on digital access and participation identifies areas where intervention is needed and using data-driven insights informs digital inclusion strategies. Digital inclusion is a critical component of ensuring equitable access to legal education, particularly as technology and AI tools become more integrated into learning environments. Without robust digital inclusion initiatives, many students may face barriers to participating fully in their education due to disparities in access to digital tools, internet connectivity and digital literacy. By prioritising initiatives that promote digital literacy, access to technology and inclusive teaching practices, legal education institutions can help bridge the digital divide and ensure that all students have the opportunity to thrive in an increasingly digital world.

3.3.1 Digital Literacy Programmes

Integrating digital literacy programmes into the curriculum equips students with the skills needed to navigate online learning environments and utilise AI tools effectively. As legal education increasingly incorporates digital and AI-driven resources, students must understand how to use these tools for legal research, case analysis and other tasks essential to their studies. These programmes should cover basic digital skills, AI tool training, and cybersecurity and data privacy awareness. Introducing students to the fundamental skills needed to operate digital devices, manage files and use software applications. This includes proficiency in using learning management systems (LMS), virtual classrooms and online libraries. Offering targeted training on how to effectively use AI-powered legal tools – such as legal research platforms, automated document analysis and predictive case outcome software – ensures that students can fully leverage the benefits of AI in their studies. Teaching students about cybersecurity

---

6 Smith (n 1).

best practices, protecting their personal data and understanding their rights and responsibilities when using digital tools. This is particularly relevant in the context of AI tools that collect and process sensitive data.

3.3.2 Educator Adaptation to Technological Advancements

Educators also play a crucial role in ensuring that students can navigate digital and AI tools effectively. Institutions must adapt continuously to technological advancements to support students. This involves professional development and incorporating AI in legal education. Offering ongoing training and support for educators to stay up to date with the latest digital tools and pedagogical methods enables them to integrate technology into their teaching and provide guidance to students effectively. Encouraging educators to integrate AI-driven tools into their teaching methods – whether through AI-assisted legal research, automated grading or simulation-based learning – can enhance the learning experience.

3.3.3 Collaborations With Local Organisations

To extend digital inclusion efforts beyond the campus, institutions can collaborate with local organisations, libraries and community centres. These partnerships can help provide access to technology and training in underserved communities, broadening digital inclusion initiatives. Some key actions include establishing community tech hubs in libraries or community centres, where students and community members can access computers, high-speed internet and training programmes; and collaborating with local organisations to offer free or low-cost digital literacy workshops which focus on essential digital skills, internet safety and AI usage.

3.3.4 Device Recycling and Donation Programmes

Institutions can reduce the digital divide by creating device recycling and donation programmes that provide students in need with access to technology. This also aligns with sustainability goals by promoting the recycling of outdated technology and reducing e-waste. Strategies include device-lending programmes and recycling outdated technology. Setting up device-lending programmes, where students can borrow laptops or tablets for the academic year or specific courses, ensures that students without access to personal devices can still participate in online learning. Encouraging students, faculty and staff to recycle outdated devices by donating them to institutions which can refurbish them and distribute them to students in need not only promotes digital inclusion but also reduces the environmental impact of electronic waste.

3.3.5 Universal Design for Learning

Institutions should embrace the principles of UDL, which emphasise flexible teaching methods that accommodate diverse learning needs, including those related to digital access. UDL aims to provide multiple means of engagement, representation and expression, ensuring that all students, regardless of their abilities or access to technology, can participate fully in their education. Implementing UDL involves multiple formats for course materials and flexible assessments. Providing course materials in various formats (e.g., text, video, audio) ensures that students with different learning preferences and access levels can choose the format that works best for them. Offering students flexibility in how they demonstrate their knowledge – whether through traditional exams, projects or digital presentations – ensures that students facing digital access challenges are not disadvantaged.

3.3.6 Student Feedback and Continuous Monitoring

Collecting feedback from students regarding their digital access challenges and experiences is essential for refining and expanding digital inclusion initiatives. Law schools should conduct regular surveys to assess students' access to digital tools and internet connectivity, as well as their comfort with using AI-driven platforms. This feedback can highlight areas where additional support or resources are needed. Institutions can also organise focus groups that bring together students from diverse backgrounds to discuss their experiences with digital learning and AI tools. This can provide deeper insights into the specific barriers faced by students from underserved communities.

3.3.7 Raising Awareness About the Digital Divide

Raising awareness about the digital divide within the legal education community is crucial for creating a culture that prioritises digital inclusion. Engaging students, faculty and staff in discussions about digital disparities and the importance of inclusion helps to foster understanding and action. Strategies include launching digital inclusion campaigns to educate the legal education community about the digital divide, highlighting the ways in which lack of access to technology can affect student success, and organising events such as workshops and seminars that bring together students, faculty and experts to discuss digital inclusion, AI accessibility and strategies for addressing disparities in access to technology.

3.3.8 Data-Driven Digital Inclusion Strategies

Continuously monitoring data on digital access and participation helps identify areas where intervention is needed and provides institutions with the information necessary to adjust and improve digital inclusion initiatives. Key actions include tracking participation rates and using data to inform strategy. Analysing data on student participation in online learning and AI-driven activities can highlight patterns of exclusion, such as lower engagement from students in rural or low-income areas. Institutions should use data-driven insights to develop targeted digital inclusion strategies. For example, if data shows that a significant number of students are accessing courses through mobile phones due to lack of computer access, the institution can prioritise mobile-friendly course materials and AI tools.

Digital inclusion initiatives are essential for ensuring that all students have equal access to the digital tools, AI technologies and online learning environments necessary for success in legal education. By promoting digital literacy, collaborating with community organisations, embracing sustainable practices like device recycling and incorporating the principles of UDL, institutions can bridge the digital divide. Continuous monitoring, feedback collection and data-driven strategies will ensure that digital inclusion efforts remain effective and responsive to student needs, ultimately fostering a more equitable and accessible legal education landscape.

Practical Tips

Mitigating the digital divide in legal education is a fundamental step in ensuring that all students have equal opportunities to benefit from AI-driven resources and online learning platforms. By combining financial support, accessibility considerations and proactive digital inclusion initiatives, institutions can create a more inclusive and equitable learning environment. The approach set out in this chapter seeks to address the digital divide in AI adoption in legal education, considering its implications for sustainability, equity and access to education. By focusing on digital inclusion initiatives, the strategy promotes educational equity and ensures that all students, regardless of their background or abilities, have equal access to AI-powered educational resources. Actionable recommendations have been proposed for mitigating the digital divide, including financial subsidies, accessibility standards adherence and digital literacy programmes, providing institutions with clear steps to promote inclusivity. While the importance of digital inclusion has been emphasised, it is also recognised that there may be potential challenges associated with upgrading technological infrastructure in institutions to support AI adoption, such as costs or technological readiness. It may also be beneficial to consider long-term sustainability considerations for bridging the digital divide, such as the scalability and adaptability of digital inclusion initiatives over time. Institutions may also face internal challenges in implementing digital inclusion initiatives, such as resistance to change or cultural barriers. Further discussion on technological infrastructure, long-term sustainability considerations and implementation challenges is therefore necessary to mitigate the digital divide

Digital Divide Mitigation 61

and enhance the effectiveness of this strategy to address sustainability ethics in relation to the adoption of AI in legal education.

While digital divide mitigation addresses key concerns in ensuring equitable access to AI-driven legal education, several challenges can arise in the implementation of these strategies.

Financial Constraints

Offering financial subsidies or device-lending programmes can be costly for institutions, especially those with limited budgets. Funding these initiatives on a large scale may require significant financial resources, which could pose challenges for sustainability in the long term. Securing discounted or subsidised internet plans requires negotiations with ISPs. The success of such collaborations may depend on the willingness of providers to offer affordable rates, particularly in rural or underserved areas where connectivity is limited.

Infrastructure Limitations

Geographic disparities in internet access can be challenging to overcome, especially in rural or remote regions where infrastructure may be insufficient. Even with subsidised internet, students in these areas may still experience slow or unreliable connectivity, hindering their ability to engage with AI-driven tools. Ensuring that all AI tools and platforms meet accessibility standards requires significant investment in infrastructure and personnel. Institutions may lack the resources or expertise to fully implement accessibility measures, particularly when integrating new AI technologies.

Cultural and Institutional Resistance

Some educators and institutions may resist adopting AI and digital tools, perceiving them as disruptive to traditional educational practices. Overcoming this resistance requires significant efforts in faculty training, awareness-building and support for integrating AI into teaching methods. Raising awareness about the digital divide and digital inclusion may be difficult in institutions that are not actively engaged in addressing these disparities. Gaining widespread buy-in from faculty, students and staff may require sustained effort and leadership support.

Maintaining Inclusivity and Accessibility

While accessibility is a key priority, it can be challenging to ensure that all AI-driven tools and resources fully adhere to standards like WCAG. Regular audits and updates are needed to maintain compliance, which can be resource intensive. Implementing UDL principles can be complex, especially in large institutions with diverse student populations. Designing flexible, accessible course materials that accommodate a range of learning styles and abilities requires continuous faculty development and institutional support.

Sustainability of Digital Literacy Programmes

Offering continuous digital literacy programmes is critical to ensuring students can effectively use AI tools. However, maintaining these programmes requires dedicated personnel, funding and resources, which may be difficult to sustain over time. As AI technologies evolve, digital literacy programmes must continuously update their content to reflect new tools, platforms and best practices. Keeping pace with these changes can strain institutional resources and requires ongoing investment.

Data Collection and Feedback Mechanisms

Collecting data on digital access and participation is essential to identify gaps, but it can be challenging to implement effective feedback mechanisms. Institutions need to develop robust systems for gathering and analysing data, which can be resource intensive. Ensuring that students actively engage in providing feedback on digital access challenges may be difficult, particularly if they are unaware of how their input will be used or if they do not see immediate improvements as a result of their feedback.

Sustainability of Device Recycling Programmes

While device recycling programmes can reduce e-waste, managing these programmes requires significant logistical effort, including refurbishing donated devices and distributing them to students. Institutions need dedicated teams to oversee these initiatives, which may require substantial resources.

Ethical and Privacy Concerns

Implementing AI tools and ensuring digital inclusion involve collecting student data, which raises concerns about privacy and security. Institutions must ensure robust data protection measures to safeguard students' personal information, which can add complexity to the digital divide mitigation efforts.

Overall, while the strategies proposed in this chapter to mitigate the digital divide are comprehensive, they face several practical challenges, including financial constraints, infrastructure limitations, resistance to change and maintaining inclusivity. Addressing these challenges requires thoughtful planning, continuous investment and strong institutional commitment to ensuring long-term sustainability in AI-driven legal education. Addressing the digital divide is essential for the long-term sustainability of AI in legal education. By implementing financial support measures, ensuring accessibility for students with disabilities and promoting proactive digital inclusion initiatives, institutions can create a more equitable learning environment. These efforts not only maximise the benefits of AI investments but also align with broader goals of sustainability by fostering educational equity and reducing environmental impacts.

4 Faculty Training and Development

Sustainable faculty development programmes play a crucial role in ensuring the long-term viability of AI initiatives in legal education. These programmes equip faculty with the knowledge and skills needed to integrate AI technologies into their teaching, research and administrative roles effectively. Ajevski and colleagues address the need to prepare law students and legal professionals for AI-powered legal practice.[1] A sustainable approach to AI in legal education involves curriculum development that not only equips students with AI skills but also incorporates discussions about the environmental and ethical aspects of AI. Bullows underscores the growing importance of digital literacy for legal professionals.[2] Faculty development programmes ensure that educators stay up to date with the latest AI technologies, tools and best practices. This allows them to continually improve their AI-related skills and knowledge. Faculty who receive proper training are better equipped to integrate AI into the curriculum and teaching methods. Zhan and colleagues emphasise the importance of innovative pedagogical approaches and engaging educational methods.[3] These considerations are pertinent when addressing the sustainability challenges of incorporating AI into legal education to ensure effective learning and long-term integration. AI integration in legal education requires pedagogical strategies that encourage hands-on learning, problem-solving and critical thinking about AI's societal, ethical and environmental implications.[4] Skilled faculty can engage in AI-related research, leading to innovations in legal education; this research contributes to the institution's reputation and relevance in the field. As AI technologies evolve, faculty development programmes enable educators to adapt and incorporate new AI tools and methods

---

1 M. Ajevski, K. Barker, A. Gilbert, L. Hardie and F. Ryan, 'ChatGPT and the Future of Legal Education and Practice' (2023) *The Law Teacher* 1.
2 A. Bullows, 'How Technology is Changing the Legal Sector' (2021) 55 *The Law Teacher* 258.
3 Z. Zhan, Y. Tong, X. Lang and B. Zhong, 'A Systematic Literature Review of Game-Based Learning in Artificial Intelligence Education' (2022) *Interactive Learning Environments* 1.
4 D. M. Ong, 'Prospects for Integrating an Environmental Sustainability Perspective within the University Law Curriculum in England' (2016) 50 *The Law Teacher* 276.

DOI: 10.4324/9781003607397-5

into their teaching and research. Sustainable faculty development programmes can embed sustainability principles into AI education; this includes promoting ethical AI practices and addressing environmental considerations in AI use.

Faculty training and development programmes in AI and data science are instrumental in preparing educators to integrate these technologies into legal education effectively; following are some strategies to accomplish this.

4.1 Offer Comprehensive Training Programmes

A structured curriculum should be developed that covers a spectrum of AI and data science topics from fundamentals to advanced concepts, including practical training modules to ensure hands-on experience. Incorporating ethics training into the curriculum to emphasise responsible AI use, ethical considerations and potential biases ensures that faculty are aware of the ethical dimensions of AI in legal education. Faculty should be equipped with strong data literacy skills, as understanding data is fundamental to AI, and provided with training on data collection, analysis and interpretation to enhance data-driven decision-making. Recognising that faculty have diverse backgrounds and skill levels, training tracks tailored to different proficiency levels should be offered, allowing educators to choose the most appropriate path. Incorporating comprehensive training programmes for faculty is essential to ensure that they are well prepared to integrate AI technologies into legal education effectively. Such programmes should be designed to enhance their understanding of AI and data science, develop practical skills and emphasise ethical considerations. This approach will empower educators to leverage AI tools responsibly, fostering a more effective and inclusive learning environment for students. Following are key components and strategies for offering these training programmes.

4.1.1 Structured Curriculum on AI and Data Science

A structured curriculum that covers a wide range of AI and data science topics is crucial. This curriculum should be designed to cater to both beginners and advanced learners, allowing faculty to gradually build their knowledge and skills. The training programme should include fundamentals of AI and data science, advanced AI topics and practical training modules. Introducing basic AI concepts – such as ML, natural language processing (NLP) and neural networks – provides faculty with a solid foundation. For those with a deeper understanding, advanced modules should focus on cutting-edge AI technologies such as deep learning, AI ethics and the integration of AI in specific areas of legal education. Law schools can offer hands-on experience with AI tools, legal technology platforms and data science applications. Faculty should have the opportunity to work on real-world case studies, simulate legal analysis using AI and experiment with AI-driven tools in a controlled environment.

Practical modules might include AI-assisted legal research tools, automated case analysis and prediction software, and AI-based grading and assessment systems.

4.1.2 Ethics Training: Emphasising Responsible AI Use

Ethics training is a critical component of any AI curriculum. With AI systems increasingly being used in education and legal practice, it is essential for faculty to understand the ethical considerations associated with AI adoption. Ethics modules should cover AI bias and fairness, data privacy and protection, transparency in AI and responsible AI use. Training should explore the potential biases in AI algorithms, such as those related to race, gender or socioeconomic status. Faculty need to understand how these biases can manifest in AI-generated outcomes and how to mitigate them. Law schools should teach faculty about the importance of safeguarding student data when using AI tools. This includes compliance with data protection regulations such as the GDPR and best practices for managing sensitive data. Institutions must encourage educators to promote transparency in the use of AI-driven tools by ensuring that students are aware of how AI systems work, what data they use and how decisions are made. Training can emphasise the ethical implications of AI-driven decision-making in legal practice, helping faculty to educate future legal professionals on the responsible use of AI in their careers.

4.1.3 Data Literacy: A Fundamental Skill

Strong data literacy skills are fundamental to understanding and using AI effectively. Faculty should be trained to collect, analyse and interpret data, as AI systems rely heavily on data inputs to generate accurate results. Key components of data literacy training include data collection and management, data analysis techniques and data-driven decision-making. Educators should learn how to collect reliable and unbiased data, how to manage large datasets and how to ensure data quality for AI applications. Law schools can provide training on basic statistical methods, data visualisation tools and data interpretation. These skills enable educators to make informed, data-driven decisions in their teaching practices. Institutions should help faculty understand how to leverage data insights to improve student outcomes, assess the effectiveness of AI-driven tools and develop evidence-based teaching strategies.

4.1.4 Tailored Training Tracks for Different Proficiency Levels

Recognising that faculty come from diverse backgrounds with varying levels of experience in technology and AI, it is important to offer tailored training tracks to accommodate their needs. Customisable training options, such as the following, will allow educators to choose the path most suitable for their skill level and learning goals.

- Beginner Track: This track should introduce basic concepts of AI, data science and ethical AI use. It is ideal for faculty with little to no experience in AI or data science.
- Intermediate Track: Faculty who already have some experience with digital tools or data analysis can engage in more in-depth AI training. This track could focus on how to integrate AI tools into their teaching and explore intermediate-level data science techniques.
- Advanced Track: For faculty with significant experience in AI or data science, the advanced track could cover cutting-edge technologies and offer training on the development or customisation of AI tools for specific legal education applications.
- Custom Learning Paths: Faculty should have the flexibility to create custom learning paths based on their specific interests, such as AI ethics, legal technology or data analytics.

4.1.5 *Workshops, Seminars and Continuous Learning*

To ensure that faculty stay updated with the latest advancements in AI, ongoing professional development opportunities should be offered. These might include workshops and seminars, mentorship and peer support, and online learning platforms. Regular workshops that focus on new AI tools, updates in legal technology or emerging trends in data science can keep educators engaged with current developments. These events should also offer networking opportunities with AI experts, legal professionals and technology developers. Law schools can create mentorship programmes through which experienced faculty can guide their peers in understanding and implementing AI tools. Peer support groups can also foster collaboration and idea sharing. Institutions should offer access to online courses and AI learning platforms, enabling faculty to learn at their own pace and explore new topics as needed.

4.1.6 *Cross-Disciplinary Collaboration and Research*

Promoting cross-disciplinary collaboration is key to fostering innovative AI applications in legal education. Encouraging partnerships among legal scholars, computer scientists, data analysts and ethicists can lead to new AI solutions to address the unique challenges of legal education. Faculty should be encouraged to collaborate with AI researchers by engaging in joint research projects with AI experts to develop tools tailored to legal education and participate in AI-focused conferences by attending or presenting at events that explore AI in education, legal practice and ethics, sharing their experiences and learning from others in the field.

4.1.7 Assessment and Feedback on Training Effectiveness

To ensure that the training programmes meet faculty needs, institutions should implement feedback mechanisms and assessment strategies such as regular surveys of faculty to gather feedback on the effectiveness of training programmes, identifying areas for improvement or additional training needs, and performance assessments to track how faculty apply AI tools and data science techniques in their teaching. Institutions should then provide constructive feedback and additional resources for faculty who may need further assistance.

Offering comprehensive training programmes is critical to ensuring that faculty are well equipped to integrate AI technologies into legal education. A structured curriculum that includes AI fundamentals, ethics training, data literacy and hands-on experience, coupled with tailored training tracks and ongoing professional development opportunities, will empower educators to use AI responsibly and effectively. By promoting cross-disciplinary collaboration, ethical AI use and continuous learning, institutions can create an environment that supports the responsible integration of AI, ultimately enhancing the quality of legal education and preparing students for a future shaped by AI technologies.

4.2 Create Communities of Practice

Ryan acknowledges the resistance that some educators and institutions may have toward adopting technology in legal education.[5] In view of this, it is important to establish communities of practice where faculty can collaborate, exchange knowledge and share best practices. These networks facilitate peer learning and support. Encouraging interdisciplinary collaboration within these communities fosters a holistic approach to AI in legal education. This can include partnerships with computer science, ethics and law faculties. Organising regular workshops, seminars and discussion forums allows faculty to showcase their AI-related projects, share insights and seek feedback from peers. Creating communities of practice is essential for fostering collaboration, knowledge sharing and innovation among educators in legal education, especially when adopting new technologies like AI. These communities serve as support networks where faculty can exchange ideas, address challenges and learn from each other's

---

[5] F. Ryan, 'Rage Against the Machine? Incorporating Legal Tech into Legal Education' (2021) 55 *The Law Teacher* 392.

experiences. By establishing these collaborative spaces, institutions can help ease the resistance that some educators and institutions may have toward adopting technology in legal education. Following are key strategies and benefits for building effective communities of practice in AI adoption.

4.2.1 Establishing Collaborative Networks

Communities of practice are built around collaborative networks where faculty from different disciplines can connect and engage in meaningful discussions about the use of AI in legal education. These networks facilitate peer learning and sharing of best practice. Faculty can learn from one another's experiences in implementing AI tools, sharing both successful strategies and challenges they encountered. Peer learning enables educators to quickly identify what works and what does not, accelerating the adoption of AI technologies. Furthermore, communities provide a platform for sharing best practices in AI adoption. This may include discussing how AI tools can enhance legal research, case analysis and classroom engagement, as well as addressing common pitfalls and ethical considerations. Communities of practice foster interdisciplinary learning by encouraging collaboration across different departments such as law, computer science, ethics and education. Faculty can gain a more holistic understanding of AI's role in legal education and explore innovative approaches to integrating AI into their teaching practices.

4.2.2 Overcoming Resistance to AI Adoption

Some educators may resist the adoption of technology due to unfamiliarity, scepticism or concerns about the impact on traditional teaching methods. Communities of practice can help mitigate this resistance by building confidence, addressing concerns and providing ongoing support. Engaging in collaborative discussions with peers who have successfully implemented AI can build confidence among hesitant educators. When faculty see tangible benefits and hear success stories from colleagues, they may be more open to experimenting with AI tools themselves. Open forums and discussion groups allow educators to voice their concerns about AI adoption. These spaces provide an opportunity to address common fears, such as AI replacing human judgement or compromising academic integrity. By collectively discussing these issues, communities of practice can find solutions and develop strategies for responsible AI use that align with legal education's values. Faculty often need support throughout the entire process of adopting new technologies. Communities of practice can offer continuous support by creating a network of mentors and peers who can provide guidance, troubleshoot problems and offer encouragement as faculty experiment with AI tools.

70 *AI and Legal Education*

4.2.3 *Encouraging Interdisciplinary Collaboration*

AI's successful integration into legal education requires interdisciplinary collaboration. Legal education faculty, computer scientists, ethicists and technologists must work together to ensure that AI tools are not only effective but also ethical and aligned with legal education's goals. Communities of practice can foster cross-disciplinary dialogue, collaborate on research projects and create AI-focused working groups. Regular meetings or virtual spaces where faculty from different disciplines can collaborate on AI-related initiatives can lead to creative and innovative approaches. Computer scientists can offer insights into AI tool development, ethicists can highlight potential concerns and legal educators can ensure that the AI aligns with pedagogical needs. Interdisciplinary teams within communities of practice can collaborate on research that explores the intersection of AI, law and education. This could lead to the development of new AI tools specifically designed for legal education or research that assesses the impact of AI on student outcomes, access to justice and ethical practice in law. Institutions can establish working groups within these communities that focus on specific areas of AI such as data ethics, legal automation or AI-enhanced learning. These groups can provide specialised knowledge and contribute to larger discussions within the community of practice.

4.2.4 *Organising Regular Workshops, Seminars and Forums*

To foster continuous learning and engagement, regular workshops, seminars and forums should be organised within communities of practice. These events offer opportunities for faculty to showcase AI-related projects, host guest speakers and experts, and facilitate group discussions. Faculty working on AI-driven initiatives can present their projects, share their progress, and receive feedback from their peers. This not only helps improve individual projects but also inspires others to pursue similar innovations. Inviting experts from fields such as AI, law, ethics and education to speak at seminars can provide fresh perspectives and introduce new ideas. Guest speakers can discuss emerging trends in AI, ethical considerations and the implications of AI in legal practice, enhancing faculty's understanding of these topics. Discussion forums provide a space for open dialogue about AI's impact on legal education. These forums allow educators to explore complex issues such as bias in AI systems, student data privacy and the use of AI in legal assessments. Faculty can debate the merits and drawbacks of various AI tools, helping to shape best practices moving forward.

4.2.5 *Creating a Culture of Innovation*

Establishing a culture of innovation within legal education is key to ensuring that AI technologies are adopted and integrated effectively. Communities of practice can foster this culture by promoting experimentation, celebrating success and encouraging thought leadership. Encouraging educators to experiment with AI tools in their teaching can lead to new insights and breakthroughs. Communities of practice should create an environment where trial and error are accepted, and where failure is viewed as a learning opportunity. Recognising and celebrating successful AI implementations within the community can motivate other faculty to adopt AI technologies. Success stories can be highlighted in newsletters, during meetings or on institutional platforms. Communities of practice can empower faculty to become thought leaders in AI and legal education. By sharing their experiences and insights through publications, presentations or workshops, faculty can contribute to the broader discourse on AI in education.

4.2.6 Leveraging Technology for Collaboration

Communities of practice can leverage digital tools to facilitate collaboration and engagement. Institutions should provide online platforms or LMS that allow faculty to share resources and best practices, communicate and collaborate, and participate in webinars and online training. Online repositories where faculty can upload resources, share lesson plans or recommend AI tools can create a central hub for knowledge sharing. Virtual discussion boards, chat groups or video conferencing tools can make it easy for faculty to collaborate on projects, ask questions and seek advice, regardless of geographic location. Offering online webinars and training sessions ensures that faculty can participate in professional development opportunities without needing to attend in person. This flexibility is particularly valuable for busy educators.

4.2.7 Feedback and Continuous Improvement

Finally, communities of practice should implement feedback mechanisms to continuously improve their effectiveness. Gathering input from participants can help refine the structure and focus of the community, ensuring that it meets the evolving needs of faculty. Feedback can be collected through surveys, questionnaires and focus groups. Regular surveys can gauge participants' satisfaction with the community of practice, identify areas for improvement and solicit suggestions for future activities. Organising focus groups with active participants can provide in-depth insights into what is working well and what needs adjustment. These groups can also help identify emerging trends or challenges related to AI adoption in legal education.

Creating communities of practice is a vital strategy for fostering collaboration, overcoming resistance to AI adoption and promoting the effective and ethical use of AI in legal education. By establishing supportive networks, encouraging interdisciplinary collaboration, organising regular workshops and seminars, and leveraging technology for communication, institutions can help faculty navigate the complexities of AI integration. These communities provide an environment where faculty can learn from each other, experiment with new technologies and contribute to the ongoing development of AI-driven legal education. Ultimately, communities of practice help build a culture of innovation that prepares educators and students alike for a future shaped by AI.

4.3 Collaborate With External Organisations

Collaborating with external AI experts and organisations to provide specialised training sessions, lectures or workshops can complement in-house training efforts. Institutions should encourage faculty to attend external conferences, webinars and training programmes related to AI in education, and to support their professional development through funding and time allowances. Forming partnerships with AI companies and legal tech firms can offer faculty insights into industry trends, real-world applications and access to cutting-edge AI tools. Exploring opportunities to offer accredited certifications or badges in collaboration with recognised AI organisations can enhance the credibility and expertise of faculty. Faculty should have access to necessary resources, including AI software datasets and computing infrastructure. Collaborating with external partners provides access to specialised resources. Establishing a continuous feedback loop with external partners and organisations keeps faculty training programmes aligned with evolving AI developments and industry standards. Regularly evaluating the impact of faculty training programmes on teaching quality, student outcomes and the integration of AI into legal education can refine and improve training initiatives. Collaborating with external organisations, particularly those with expertise in AI, offers a powerful way for legal education institutions to complement their in-house training efforts and provide faculty with the latest insights, tools and resources for AI integration. This collaborative approach fosters continuous professional development, keeping educators up to date with the evolving landscape of AI in both education and the legal profession.

4.3.1 Specialised Training Sessions and Workshops

Partnering with external AI experts and organisations enables institutions to host specialised training sessions, lectures or workshops that deliver targeted knowledge in areas where in-house resources may be limited. External experts can offer advanced AI knowledge and hands-on training. External AI professionals can introduce faculty to advanced AI topics, such as ML, NLP and deep learning. These insights help faculty understand the technical aspects of AI, which can then be applied in legal education settings. Workshops facilitated by AI companies or research institutions can provide hands-on experience with the latest AI tools and platforms. Faculty benefit from practical learning opportunities, allowing them to engage directly with cutting-edge technologies. By collaborating with external partners, institutions can ensure their training programmes remain comprehensive and aligned with current AI trends and practices.

4.3.2 Encouraging Faculty to Attend External Conferences and Training

Institutions should actively encourage faculty to attend external conferences, webinars and training programmes related to AI and its application in education. This professional development can be supported through funding and time allowances, networking opportunities and exposure to AI in practice. Providing financial support for travel, conference fees or workshop registrations demonstrates institutional commitment to faculty development. Time allowances also ensure that faculty can attend events without feeling burdened by their regular teaching duties. External conferences and events allow faculty to network with AI experts, researchers and educators from other institutions. These networking opportunities can lead to new ideas, collaborations and innovations in AI adoption within legal education. External conferences often highlight real-world AI applications in various sectors, including law. By attending these events, faculty gain a broader understanding of how AI is transforming the legal industry, which can inform how they teach future legal professionals.

4.3.3 Partnerships With AI Companies and Legal Tech Firms

Forming partnerships with AI companies and legal tech firms offers faculty access to the latest industry trends, tools and AI-driven legal applications. These partnerships can lead to real-world insights, access to cutting-edge AI tools and industry-driven research projects. Collaborating with legal tech firms enables faculty to understand how AI is being used in legal practice, from predictive analytics in case law to AI-driven contract analysis. This knowledge can be incorporated into curricula, preparing students for the AI-driven legal landscape. AI companies can provide faculty with access to the latest software, platforms and datasets. Faculty can use these resources to experiment with AI applications in teaching, legal research and case analysis. Collaborations between legal education institutions and AI companies can result in joint research projects that explore the intersection of AI and law. These projects can lead to innovative solutions and tools that benefit both legal practitioners and educators. Partnerships with external AI organisations not only provide faculty with practical resources but also help them stay informed about how AI is shaping the future of the legal profession.

74 *AI and Legal Education*

4.3.4 Accredited Certifications and Badges

Offering accredited certifications or digital badges in collaboration with recognised AI organisations can enhance faculty's credibility and expertise. These certifications can serve as a formal acknowledgement of a faculty member's proficiency in AI and legal technology. To facilitate this, institutions can collaborate with renowned AI organisations, incorporate certifications into faculty training and enhance faculty credibility. By partnering with well-established AI organisations or training platforms, institutions can offer certifications that carry industry recognition, adding value to faculty's professional development. Institutions can integrate certification opportunities within their AI training programmes. Faculty who complete these certifications can demonstrate their expertise in AI tools, ethics and legal technology to both peers and students. Certified faculty are more likely to be perceived as knowledgeable leaders in AI integration. This credibility can attract students interested in AI-driven legal education and increase the institution's overall standing in the academic community.

4.3.5 Providing Necessary Resources for AI Integration

For faculty to adopt AI in legal education effectively, they need access to critical resources, including AI software, datasets and computing infrastructure. Collaborating with external partners can help institutions acquire these resources. Partnerships with AI firms can grant faculty access to proprietary software or platforms designed for AI research, data analysis or legal automation. Faculty can use these tools to enhance teaching, research and student engagement. Legal education often requires specific datasets, such as legal documents, case law or court records. Collaborating with legal tech companies or AI organisations can provide faculty with access to high-quality datasets for training AI models or conducting legal research. AI development requires robust computing power. Institutions can collaborate with technology firms or cloud service providers to offer faculty access to advanced computing infrastructure, enabling them to develop and run AI models efficiently.

4.3.6 Continuous Feedback Loops With External Partners

Establishing continuous feedback loops with external partners ensures that training programmes remain aligned with evolving AI developments and industry standards. By maintaining regular communication and evaluation, institutions can stay current with AI trends, adapt to industry changes and maintain high standards. External partners can provide timely updates on the latest advancements in AI, ensuring that faculty training remains relevant and effective. As AI technology evolves, so do its applications in law and education. By collaborating with AI experts, institutions can adjust their training curricula to reflect the changing landscape and emerging ethical considerations. Continuous feedback from external organisations helps institutions maintain high standards in their AI-related training, ensuring that faculty are equipped with the skills and knowledge necessary to integrate AI into legal education successfully.

4.3.7 Evaluating the Impact of Training Programmes

Regularly evaluating the impact of faculty training programmes on teaching quality, student outcomes and the integration of AI into legal education is essential for refining and improving these initiatives. Institutions can collaborate with external partners to evaluate how AI training affects the way faculty teach; assess whether students in AI-integrated legal education programmes perform better in areas like legal research, problem-solving or understanding AI's role in law; and evaluate how well AI has been integrated into legal education programmes. This data can help measure the effectiveness of faculty training. By regularly evaluating training initiatives, institutions can continuously improve their efforts, ensuring that AI adoption in legal education is both effective and sustainable.

Collaborating with external organisations is a key strategy for legal education institutions aiming to enhance faculty training on AI. By leveraging external expertise, attending AI-focused conferences, forming partnerships with AI and legal tech companies, and offering accredited certifications, institutions can equip their faculty with the skills and knowledge necessary to integrate AI into their teaching and research. Additionally, providing necessary resources, establishing continuous feedback loops with external partners and evaluating the impact of training programmes are all crucial for ensuring that AI adoption aligns with industry trends and improves educational outcomes. Ultimately, these collaborations will help legal education institutions remain at the forefront of AI-driven innovation.

Practical Tips

Faculty training and development programmes in AI not only enhance educators' capabilities but also contribute to the advancement of legal education. They create a culture of innovation, ethical AI use and interdisciplinary collaboration, ensuring that AI initiatives align with educational and sustainability goals in the long term. Faculty development programmes have a crucial role in ensuring the long-term viability of AI initiatives in legal education. Providing faculty with training on AI technologies, tools and best practices ensures that educators are equipped to integrate AI into the curriculum effectively. This skill enhancement is essential for keeping up with the evolving landscape of AI in legal education. Faculty development programmes encourage educators to engage in AI-related research, leading to innovations in legal education. This research contributes to the institution's reputation and relevance in the field while addressing sustainability challenges through ethical AI practices and environmental considerations. Establishing communities of practice fosters collaboration, knowledge exchange and peer support among faculty. Interdisciplinary collaboration promotes a holistic approach to AI in legal education and allows for partnerships with relevant faculties, such as computer science, ethics and law. By creating a culture of innovation, ethical AI use and interdisciplinary collaboration, faculty development programmes contribute to the advancement of legal education and ensure that AI initiatives align with educational and sustainability goals in the long term.

However, overcoming resistance among some educators and institutions toward adopting technology in legal education requires tailored approaches and support mechanisms. In addition, the implementation of faculty development programmes requires significant resources, including time, funding and expertise. Institutions with limited resources may struggle to establish comprehensive programmes, hindering the widespread adoption of AI in legal education. While collaboration and networking are essential components of faculty development programmes, sustaining these efforts in the long term can be challenging. Without proper support and incentives, interdisciplinary collaboration may diminish over time. Finally, although faculty development programmes aim to enable educators to adapt to evolving AI technologies, keeping pace with rapid advancements remains a challenge. Continuous training and updates are necessary to ensure educators remain proficient in integrating new AI tools and methods into their teaching and research. The challenges associated with the implementation of faculty training and development programmes for AI integration in legal education include several factors across various domains, including the following.

Resource Constraints

Developing comprehensive training programmes can be resource intensive. Institutions may struggle with the financial burden of offering structured, hands-on training that covers a broad range of AI topics. Providing continuous education and access to evolving AI tools could add further financial strain. Faculty may lack access to the necessary software, computing resources or data needed for effective training. Building or acquiring such infrastructure can be costly and may require collaboration with external partners, which may not always be feasible.

Diverse Faculty Skill Levels

Faculty often come from diverse backgrounds and have different levels of familiarity with AI technologies. Designing training programmes that cater to both novice users and advanced practitioners presents a challenge, as each group will have different needs and learning curves. Some educators may resist adopting AI technologies due to discomfort with digital tools, scepticism about AI's role in legal education or fear of technology replacing traditional pedagogical methods. Overcoming this resistance requires cultural change and support mechanisms within institutions.

Sustainability and Long-Term Adaptation

AI technologies are rapidly evolving, and keeping up with these changes poses a challenge for long-term sustainability. Continuous updates to faculty training programmes – which may require frequent curriculum revisions and additional investment in time and resources – will be necessary. Ensuring that training programmes stay relevant as AI technologies and their applications in legal education evolve is another challenge. Faculty development programmes must be dynamic and capable of adapting to new trends and technologies, which requires long-term planning and flexibility.

Ethical and Societal Considerations

As part of AI training, faculty need to understand the ethical implications of AI use, including issues related to bias, fairness and privacy. These are complex topics that may require interdisciplinary collaboration, further complicating the design of training programmes. Embedding sustainability principles into AI training programmes – such as promoting ethical AI use and considering the environmental impact of AI – adds an additional layer of complexity to faculty training, especially if faculty are unfamiliar with these broader issues.

Collaboration and Interdisciplinary Engagement

Establishing communities of practice that foster collaboration and peer learning can be difficult to sustain over time. Ensuring active participation from faculty across disciplines requires consistent support, leadership and engagement. While collaborating with external AI experts and organisations can bring valuable insights, coordinating such partnerships can be logistically challenging. Securing funding, managing these relationships and aligning training goals with industry standards and educational priorities can be complex.

Measuring Impact and Effectiveness

Regular evaluation of the effectiveness of faculty training programmes is essential, but assessing the impact on teaching quality, student outcomes and AI integration poses a challenge. Developing objective metrics and collecting relevant data to measure these aspects may require significant effort. Encouraging faculty to continuously apply AI-related knowledge in their teaching and research can be difficult. Without proper follow-up or incentives, there may be a lack of sustained adoption of AI technologies in educational practice.

The main challenges in faculty training and development for AI integration in legal education include resource limitations, diverse faculty skill levels, resistance to change and keeping up with evolving technology. Additionally, addressing ethical concerns, fostering collaboration and measuring the effectiveness of training programmes are complex tasks that require careful planning and ongoing support from institutions. Faculty training and development programmes in AI are vital for equipping educators with the skills necessary to integrate AI technologies into legal education effectively. These programmes not only enhance individual capabilities but also contribute to the institution's reputation and the advancement of legal education as a whole. By fostering a culture of innovation, promoting ethical AI use and encouraging interdisciplinary collaboration, these programmes ensure that AI initiatives align with long-term educational and sustainability goals. Through comprehensive training, the creation of communities of practice and collaborations with external organisations, legal education institutions can position themselves at the forefront of AI integration, ultimately benefiting students, faculty and society.

5 Regulatory Compliance in AI Adoption

The importance of sustainability literacy in professional training has been mentioned already in this book. Reid has argued for the integration of Education for Sustainable Development (ESD)[1] principles into professional curricula, including legal education.[2] Similarly, addressing the impact of AI in legal education requires preparing students and faculty with the necessary knowledge and literacy to navigate the ethical, environmental and legal dimensions of AI adoption. Agrawal emphasises the need for appropriate governance and regulations when implementing AI.[3] However, navigating the evolving legal and regulatory landscape related to AI in education can be challenging. Staying compliant with data protection laws and AI ethics regulations is crucial for sustainability and avoiding legal issues. Compliance with data protection laws, such as the GDPR in Europe, is essential. Legal education institutions must manage and protect student data in accordance with these laws, which often have stringent requirements. AI ethics regulations and guidelines are continually evolving; keeping up with these changes and ensuring that AI initiatives align with ethical principles can be challenging, but is crucial to avoid ethical and legal pitfalls. International compliance adds complexity to AI adoption: institutions with a global reach may need to navigate varying regulatory landscapes in different countries. Legal education often involves the use of copyrighted materials, and institutions must thus ensure that AI-generated content or tools do not infringe upon IP rights. Regulatory compliance is an intricate challenge that requires law schools to stay vigilant and proactive in addressing the evolving landscape of AI-related regulations and ethical standards.

To ensure sustainability and legal integrity, institutions should adopt a comprehensive approach to compliance, encompassing the following strategies.

---

1 UNESCO, 'Education for Sustainable Development' (2023) <www.unesco.org/en/education-sustainable-development>.
2 C. T. Reid, 'Education for Sustainable Development and the Professional Curriculum' (2016) 50 *The Law Teacher* 300.
3 K. P. Agrawal, 'Towards Adoption of Generative AI in Organisational Settings' (2023) *Journal of Computer Information Systems* 1.

DOI: 10.4324/9781003607397-6

5.1 Continuous Regulatory Awareness

A dedicated team or individual responsible for monitoring changes in AI-related regulations should be maintained at the local, national and international levels. Universities should stay informed about updates to data protection laws, AI ethics guidelines and other relevant regulations, establish a system for regular updates and dissemination of regulatory information within the institution and ensure that relevant staff and stakeholders are well informed about the latest developments. Maintaining continuous regulatory awareness is essential for universities and legal education institutions that seek to integrate AI into their academic, administrative and research practices. As AI regulations and ethical standards evolve rapidly at the local, national and international levels, institutions must establish dedicated systems to keep pace with these changes. Failure to do so can result in non-compliance, legal risks and reputational damage. A well-organised approach to regulatory awareness ensures that universities can adopt AI technologies responsibly and ethically while protecting the rights of students, staff and other stakeholders.

5.1.1 Dedicated Regulatory Monitoring Teams

To ensure proactive compliance with evolving AI regulations, universities should establish dedicated teams or designate individuals whose sole responsibility is to monitor changes in AI-related laws and policies. These teams should track local, national and international regulations. AI-related regulations vary significantly across jurisdictions, making it essential for institutions to monitor legal developments at multiple levels. Teams should track local data protection laws, national regulations concerning AI ethics and international guidelines such as the GDPR in Europe or AI regulatory frameworks from global organisations like the United Nations Educational, Scientific and Cultural Organization (UNESCO) and the Organisation for Economic Co-Operation and Development (OECD). As ethical considerations around AI continue to evolve, monitoring changes to ethical guidelines related to bias, fairness, transparency and accountability is crucial. The team should also stay updated on changes in data protection laws, ensuring that any AI implementation respects privacy rights and data security protocols. Regulatory monitoring teams should maintain strong relationships with legal experts, either in-house or through external partnerships, to interpret complex regulations and assess their implications for AI adoption. Legal experts can offer guidance on how best to comply with regulatory changes and mitigate legal risks associated with AI.

5.1.2 Establish a System for Regular Updates

Universities must create a systematic process for staying up to date with regulatory changes and disseminating relevant information throughout the institution. This system should be structured to receive real-time updates, regular reports and bulletins, and tailored communication. Regulatory monitoring teams should subscribe to updates from regulatory bodies, industry groups and government agencies to receive real-time notifications about changes in AI laws, guidelines and ethics standards. A system for creating and distributing regular regulatory updates (monthly, quarterly or biannually) ensures that faculty, administrative staff and other key stakeholders are informed consistently about relevant legal changes. These updates should cover various aspects of AI adoption, including data privacy, IP and ethical AI use. The information provided should be tailored to different departments or stakeholders based on their specific needs. For example, IT departments may need to focus on cybersecurity and data protection regulations, while academic departments may need information about the ethical implications of AI in teaching and research.

5.1.3 Engaging Stakeholders With Regulatory Developments

Beyond regular updates, it is essential to engage stakeholders actively in understanding the implications of regulatory changes for their roles. This can be done through workshops and seminars, internal training programmes and departmental liaisons. Hosting workshops, seminars or webinars led by legal and regulatory experts helps faculty and staff better understand new AI regulations. These events can cover a range of topics, from data privacy compliance to ethical considerations in AI applications. To ensure that all relevant personnel are fully aware of the latest developments, universities should implement mandatory training programmes that focus on key regulatory areas such as GDPR compliance, AI ethics and IP rights. These programmes ensure that both faculty and administrators are equipped to navigate the evolving legal landscape. Appointing regulatory liaisons within each department allows for more targeted dissemination of information. These individuals can act as intermediaries, ensuring that regulatory changes are communicated efficiently to department members and that feedback or questions are conveyed back to the regulatory monitoring team.

5.1.4 AI Compliance in Global Contexts

Many universities and legal education institutions operate across borders, either through international collaborations, research partnerships or online learning programmes. As such, maintaining awareness of regulatory developments in multiple jurisdictions is critical for international compliance. AI regulation varies widely between countries. For example, the EU's GDPR imposes stringent data protection standards, while the United States has a more fragmented regulatory approach. Institutions must be aware of which regulations apply to their operations, particularly if they have students, faculty or research collaborations in different countries. For institutions handling cross-border data transfers, awareness of data protection regulations in each country is essential. Universities should monitor data localisation requirements or restrictions on sharing personal information across borders, ensuring that they comply with international data transfer laws. Institutions should engage with global AI ethics standards set by organisations like the European Commission, UNESCO or OECD. Aligning with these standards helps ensure that AI implementations adhere to universal ethical principles while allowing for compliance with local laws.

5.1.5 Leveraging Technology for Regulatory Awareness

Technology can play a pivotal role in monitoring and managing regulatory compliance. Universities can leverage AI and other technological tools to assist with automated compliance monitoring, compliance dashboards and data protection tools. AI-driven tools can be used to automatically monitor regulatory databases, legal announcements and government updates, flagging any changes that may affect the institution. These tools reduce the burden on human staff and ensure real-time monitoring. Developing compliance dashboards that track the institution's adherence to various regulations helps provide an at-a-glance overview of compliance levels. These dashboards can be shared with stakeholders to ensure ongoing awareness and transparency. AI tools can also assist with data protection by monitoring data usage across the institution to ensure that it complies with laws such as GDPR. These tools can identify potential breaches, notify relevant personnel and offer suggestions for corrective actions.

5.1.6 Staying Ahead of AI Regulatory Trends

As AI is a rapidly advancing field, regulatory trends can change quickly. Institutions must focus on predictive regulatory awareness by anticipating future regulations, participating in policy discussions and adapting institutional policies. Engaging with thought leaders, policy advisers and regulatory bodies allows universities to anticipate future AI regulations before they are enacted. This foresight enables institutions to prepare proactively, rather than reacting after regulations have taken effect. Universities can also participate actively in policy-making discussions. By contributing to the development of AI regulations, institutions can influence future laws to ensure they consider the needs and challenges faced by academic institutions in AI adoption. Law schools should update internal AI policies and frameworks regularly to reflect both current and anticipated regulatory changes. This flexibility ensures that the institution remains compliant with evolving laws and guidelines, protecting it from legal risks and enhancing its reputation for responsible AI use.

Continuous regulatory awareness is a crucial aspect of successfully integrating AI into legal education and broader academic institutions. By establishing dedicated teams to monitor changes in regulations, developing systematic communication processes, engaging stakeholders and leveraging technology, universities can ensure they remain compliant with evolving AI laws and ethical guidelines. Furthermore, staying informed about international regulations and anticipating future legal developments positions institutions to adopt AI responsibly while safeguarding the rights of their students, faculty and broader communities.

5.2 Legal Expertise and Consultation

Engaging legal experts or consultants with expertise in data protection, IP and AI ethics can provide guidance on compliance measures, help interpret complex regulations and offer strategic advice. Conducting legal audits or assessments of AI initiatives with the assistance of legal experts can identify potential compliance gaps and provide recommendations for remediation. Engaging legal experts and consultants is a critical component of ensuring that AI adoption within legal education institutions aligns with the complex and evolving landscape of data protection, IP and AI ethics regulations. AI technologies introduce new legal and ethical challenges, and institutions must navigate these with precision to avoid potential pitfalls. By leveraging legal expertise, institutions can receive comprehensive guidance on compliance, mitigate risks and ensure that AI initiatives uphold the highest ethical and legal standards.

5.2.1 Expertise in Data Protection and Privacy Laws

One of the primary areas where legal expertise is crucial is data protection and privacy laws. AI systems often involve handling large volumes of personal data, including sensitive information, which must be managed in compliance with regulations such as the GDPR in Europe, the CCPA in the United States and other regional or national privacy laws. Legal experts help institutions interpret complex data protection regulations and apply them to AI projects. This ensures that AI systems adhere to requirements such as lawful data collection, informed consent, anonymisation and the rights of individuals regarding their data. Consultants with expertise in data privacy can offer best practices for managing student and faculty data, ensuring that AI systems only use data in ways that comply with legal obligations. This includes recommendations on secure data storage, transfer protocols and deletion policies. If an institution operates across borders, legal experts are essential for advising on cross-border data transfers. They help ensure that AI systems and data exchanges comply with international data protection laws, such as those governing the transfer of data between the EU and the United States.

5.2.2 Intellectual Property Considerations

AI technologies introduce complex issues related to IP rights, particularly when it comes to AI-generated content, the use of third-party data and the ownership of AI models. Legal experts can clarify ownership rights over content created by AI systems. This is particularly important in educational settings where AI tools may generate educational content, assessments or other intellectual outputs. Institutions need clear guidelines on who holds the rights to these creations – whether it is the institution, the creators of the AI or the users. Legal consultants can assist in licensing agreements for AI tools and datasets, ensuring that institutions respect the IP rights of third-party developers or content creators. This includes advice on licensing open-source AI software and ensuring compliance with copyright laws. For institutions developing proprietary AI systems or tools, legal experts can provide strategies for protecting IP through patents, trademarks or copyrights. They can also offer guidance on preventing unauthorised use of the institution's AI technologies.

5.2.3 AI Ethics and Compliance

Navigating the ethical considerations of AI in legal education requires ongoing consultation with experts in AI ethics. These experts help ensure that AI tools and systems used in academic settings are aligned with ethical principles such as fairness, accountability and transparency. Legal experts with AI ethics expertise can assist in evaluating AI systems for compliance with ethical guidelines, ensuring that the institution's AI applications are free from bias and discriminatory practices. This is critical in educational contexts where fairness and inclusivity are paramount. Legal consultants can offer advice on bias mitigation strategies, helping institutions identify potential biases in AI systems and recommending legal and ethical safeguards. For instance, they can review training data and algorithms to ensure diverse representation and fair outcomes for all student demographics. Legal and ethical consultants can help establish transparency measures for AI tools, advising on ways to make AI decision-making processes explainable and accountable. This includes recommending transparency reports and user consent protocols that adhere to ethical standards.

5.2.4 Legal Audits and Risk Assessments

Regular legal audits or risk assessments conducted by legal experts are invaluable in identifying potential compliance gaps in AI initiatives. These audits involve thorough evaluations of the institution's AI systems and their adherence to applicable laws and ethical guidelines. Legal experts can conduct system-wide audits to evaluate whether AI technologies are compliant with current regulations. This includes reviewing data collection practices, consent mechanisms, data security protocols and algorithmic decision-making processes. Through detailed assessments, legal consultants can identify areas where compliance may be lacking or where institutional practices are at risk of violating data protection, IP or AI ethics regulations. For example, they may discover that an AI system inadvertently collects more personal data than necessary or that transparency in decision-making is insufficient. After conducting audits, legal experts provide actionable recommendations for addressing compliance gaps. This could involve updating data privacy policies, adjusting AI algorithms to eliminate bias or implementing new security measures to protect sensitive data.

5.2.5 Strategic Legal Advice on AI Adoption

Legal experts and consultants also offer strategic advice on AI adoption, helping institutions make informed decisions about the integration of AI technologies into their operations. Their advice extends beyond compliance to include risk management and long-term planning. Legal experts can help institutions develop risk mitigation strategies for AI adoption, advising on how to address potential legal liabilities such as data breaches, IP disputes or ethical violations. When partnering with external AI vendors or developers, legal consultants assist with contract negotiations, ensuring that the institution's rights and responsibilities are clearly defined. They help structure agreements that address data protection, IP ownership and liability issues. Legal experts can help institutions develop AI policies that align with both regulatory and ethical standards. This includes drafting data protection policies, terms of service for AI tools and guidelines for the responsible use of AI in education.

5.2.6 Ongoing Legal Consultation

Given the rapidly evolving nature of AI-related laws and guidelines, ongoing consultation with legal experts is essential. Institutions should engage in continuous legal consultation to stay ahead of regulatory changes and ensure that AI initiatives remain compliant as new regulations emerge. Legal consultants can provide regular updates on changes to AI-related laws, such as new data privacy regulations or ethical guidelines for AI. These updates ensure that institutions can adjust their AI strategies in response to legal developments. Legal experts can assist institutions in scenario planning, helping them anticipate potential legal challenges and prepare for future regulatory changes. This proactive approach enables institutions to adjust their AI initiatives to minimise legal risks. Legal consultants provide critical support in the event of legal challenges such as data breaches, IP disputes or regulatory investigations. They can assist with crisis management, including responding to legal claims, preparing for audits or negotiating settlements.

Engaging legal expertise and consultation is an essential strategy for any institution looking to adopt AI responsibly and ethically. By working with legal experts, institutions can navigate the complex regulatory landscape surrounding data protection, IP and AI ethics, ensuring that AI initiatives are both legally compliant and ethically sound. Legal consultants offer critical guidance on compliance measures, conduct audits to identify potential risks and provide strategic advice to ensure the successful and responsible integration of AI technologies into legal education. Continuous engagement with legal experts ensures that institutions can stay ahead of regulatory changes and address any legal challenges that arise in the dynamic field of AI.

5.3 Compliance Framework

Developing a comprehensive compliance framework which outlines the institution's approach to adhering to regulations and ethical standards related to AI should encompass data protection, ethical considerations and other relevant compliance areas. Institutions should implement monitoring mechanisms within the compliance framework to track AI initiatives and ensure that they remain in alignment with regulations, review and update compliance protocols regularly to reflect changes in the legal landscape, and define clear reporting procedures for incidents or issues related to regulatory compliance. Staff and stakeholders should be encouraged to report compliance concerns promptly so that they can be addressed in a timely manner. A comprehensive compliance framework is essential for legal education institutions to manage the challenges posed by the adoption of AI technologies. This framework serves as a structured approach to ensure that the institution adheres to relevant regulations and ethical standards across multiple domains, including data protection, ethical AI use, IP and transparency. By developing such a framework, institutions can create a robust system to proactively manage legal and ethical obligations while fostering a culture of accountability.

5.3.1 Core Components of the Compliance Framework

The framework should address several key areas, ensuring that all aspects of AI adoption are covered. Compliance with data protection laws such as the GDPR, the CCPA or other local and international privacy regulations is a critical component. The framework should outline protocols for data collection, storage, processing, consent management and data security. Institutions must establish data handling guidelines that ensure student and faculty data is treated with confidentiality and used only for intended purposes. Special attention should be given to the processing of sensitive personal data, ensuring that AI systems only use data in ways that comply with the law. Ensuring that AI technologies are aligned with ethical principles such as fairness, accountability, transparency and non-discrimination is vital. The compliance framework should include protocols to monitor AI systems for bias, ensuring that AI algorithms do not perpetuate discrimination or unequal treatment of students or faculty. Institutions should also ensure that the framework outlines the ethical use of AI in the assessment and grading of students, avoiding any undue reliance on AI that might compromise fairness. Legal education institutions often use or create AI tools that involve IP. The framework should specify how AI-generated content, datasets and tools are licensed or patented. Clear guidelines should be established regarding the use of copyrighted materials within AI systems, ensuring that AI does not infringe on IP rights.

5.3.2 *Monitoring Mechanisms for AI Initiatives*

A well-structured compliance framework should incorporate monitoring mechanisms to continuously track AI initiatives and ensure that they remain compliant with relevant regulations and ethical guidelines. Institutions can implement automated monitoring tools that review AI systems regularly for compliance with data protection laws, ethical guidelines and other relevant regulations. These tools can be used to audit algorithmic decision-making processes, identify potential biases and monitor data use across AI initiatives. In addition to automated tools, human oversight is essential for continuous compliance monitoring. Ethics committees or compliance review boards should be established to oversee AI initiatives and ensure that they align with both legal and ethical standards. These committees can evaluate new AI projects before deployment and conduct periodic reviews to address any emerging compliance concerns. Staff and stakeholders should be required to report regularly on the status of AI projects and any potential compliance risks. This process helps ensure accountability and keeps everyone informed about potential issues that may require remediation.

5.3.3 *Updating Compliance Protocols*

The compliance framework should include protocols for reviewing and updating institutional policies regularly, ensuring that they reflect changes in the legal and ethical landscape. As AI-related regulations continue to evolve, institutions must adapt to maintain compliance. The institution must establish a system for monitoring changes in AI-related laws, data protection regulations and ethical standards. A dedicated team or designated individual should be tasked with keeping the institution up to date on changes at the local, national and international levels. This person or group should disseminate information frequently to relevant stakeholders and departments to ensure they remain informed. Scheduled policy reviews should be built into the compliance framework to ensure that institutional guidelines align with the latest regulatory developments. For example, new data privacy laws may necessitate updates to consent protocols or security measures, while emerging AI ethics guidelines might require adjustments to how AI systems are deployed in educational settings.

5.3.4 Incident Reporting and Response Procedures

The framework should also include clear procedures for reporting and addressing compliance issues as they arise. Prompt action is essential to mitigate risks and avoid potential legal or ethical violations. Institutions must establish clear reporting channels for staff, faculty and students to raise concerns about compliance issues. These channels should be accessible and well publicised, ensuring that individuals can easily report issues related to data protection, bias, IP infringement or other ethical concerns. In the event of a compliance breach, the framework should outline the steps for incident management and remediation. This could include internal investigations, legal consultation and corrective actions to ensure that compliance is restored and future breaches are prevented. Incident management should also include a feedback loop whereby the causes of the breach are identified, and the compliance framework should be updated to address any gaps or weaknesses.

5.3.5 Promoting a Culture of Compliance

Building a culture where compliance with regulations and ethical standards is valued and prioritised is critical to the success of the framework. Faculty, staff and students should be trained repeatedly on the importance of regulatory and ethical compliance, especially as it relates to AI use in legal education. Compliance training should cover data protection laws, IP rights, AI ethics and bias detection, among other relevant topics. Institutions should provide ongoing education on the evolving regulatory landscape, helping staff stay informed about new requirements and best practices. A whistleblower protection policy should be implemented to encourage individuals to report compliance concerns without fear of retaliation. This creates an environment where compliance issues can be addressed promptly and transparently.

5.3.6 Compliance Audits

Periodic internal audits of the institution's AI systems and policies should be conducted to ensure that all compliance measures are functioning effectively. A regular audit schedule should be established, where internal auditors or compliance officers evaluate AI initiatives for adherence to data protection regulations, IP guidelines and ethical standards. These audits help identify compliance gaps early, enabling institutions to address issues before they escalate into legal or ethical violations. In addition to internal audits, institutions may consider engaging external auditors to provide an independent assessment of their AI compliance framework. External audits can offer valuable insights and ensure that institutional practices align with industry best practices and legal standards.

A comprehensive compliance framework is an essential tool for legal education institutions seeking to responsibly integrate AI technologies. By addressing data protection, ethical considerations and IP issues, this framework provides a structured approach to ensuring that AI initiatives remain compliant with evolving regulations and ethical standards. Regular monitoring, incident reporting, continuous education and internal audits are key components of an effective compliance framework, helping institutions maintain accountability and transparency while mitigating legal risks. Ultimately, this framework fosters a culture of compliance that supports responsible and ethical AI adoption in legal education.

Practical Tips

Regulatory compliance in AI adoption for legal education is an ongoing and complicated endeavour. Legal education institutions must invest in staying informed, engaging legal expertise and establishing robust compliance frameworks to ensure sustainability and ethical integrity in AI initiatives. Compliance efforts should align with institutional values and prioritise the protection of student data and ethical AI practices. The preceding section emphasised the importance of regulatory compliance in AI adoption, particularly in legal education. Highlighting the need to adhere to data protection laws, AI ethics regulations and copyright laws ensure that legal education institutions are aware of their legal responsibilities. Compliance with data protection laws and AI ethics regulations is crucial for maintaining legal integrity and avoiding ethical and legal issues. Promoting regulatory compliance contributes to sustainability and ethical integrity in AI initiatives within legal education. Acknowledging the complexity of international compliance adds depth to this strategy. Institutions with a global reach must navigate varying regulatory landscapes, and addressing this challenge demonstrates a comprehensive approach to regulatory compliance. Institutions must stay vigilant and proactive in addressing the evolving regulatory landscape of AI-related regulations and ethical standards. By investing in staying informed, engaging legal expertise and establishing robust compliance frameworks, institutions can ensure sustainability and ethical integrity in AI initiatives. Aligning compliance efforts with institutional values and prioritising the protection of student data and ethical AI practices is crucial. This alignment ensures that regulatory compliance efforts are integrated into the broader mission and values of the institution.

However, maintaining regulatory compliance requires significant resources, including time, expertise and financial investment. Institutions with limited resources may struggle to allocate sufficient resources to stay informed, engage legal expertise and establish robust compliance frameworks. Furthermore, keeping up with changes in data protection laws, AI ethics regulations and copyright laws requires ongoing effort and resources, posing a challenge for institutions. Addressing the challenge of how institutions can effectively navigate varying regulatory landscapes in different countries may require tailored approaches and expertise in international law. Engaging legal expertise is therefore essential for ensuring regulatory compliance, but institutions may face challenges in accessing and affording such expertise. Dependence on external legal counsel may introduce additional costs and dependencies. Institutions may also struggle to adapt to changes in regulations, leading to compliance gaps and potential legal risks. Several challenges are inherent in the regulatory compliance of AI adoption in legal education, as outlined in what follows.

Keeping Up With Rapidly Evolving AI Regulations

AI regulations are still in development, and institutions may face difficulty staying current with changes. With AI ethics guidelines, data protection laws and sector-specific regulations constantly evolving, maintaining compliance can be overwhelming. The need for institutions to adapt quickly to new laws poses a sustainability challenge. Institutions with a global presence need to navigate multiple – and often conflicting – regulatory frameworks. Managing compliance across different countries with varying standards for data protection (e.g., GDPR versus local laws) adds complexity to AI adoption.

Data Protection and Privacy Issues

Legal education institutions need to handle vast amounts of sensitive data. Ensuring the security and privacy of this data, particularly when AI tools are involved, is challenging. Meeting strict data protection regulations like the GDPR requires strong data governance structures which can be difficult to implement and monitor. Institutions risk significant legal and reputational damage if data breaches occur. This is especially true with AI systems that involve cloud-based solutions and large-scale data processing, increasing the risk of mishandling personal information.

AI Ethics and Bias Management

Ensuring that AI tools used in legal education do not perpetuate biases in assessments or decision-making is a key ethical and regulatory challenge.

AI systems trained on biased data can unintentionally discriminate, which could lead to legal consequences and ethical concerns. AI algorithms often operate as "black boxes," making it hard to explain how decisions are reached. Legal institutions must navigate the ethical requirement of transparency, balancing innovation with the need to provide clear explanations for AI-generated outcomes.

Intellectual Property Rights

AI-generated content in legal education may raise questions about IP ownership. Institutions need to ensure that AI tools do not infringe upon existing copyrights and that proper licensing agreements are in place. There is ongoing debate about who owns the rights to AI-generated work – whether it is the institution, individual faculty or the AI developers. Legal institutions must navigate this uncertainty to avoid potential IP disputes.

Resource and Expertise Constraints

Institutions may lack the in-house legal expertise to navigate the complexities of AI regulations and data protection laws. Engaging external experts can be costly, and smaller institutions may not have the resources to conduct legal audits or assessments. Maintaining continuous vigilance over AI initiatives, monitoring compliance and updating policies in response to regulatory changes can be resource intensive. Smaller or underfunded institutions may struggle to allocate the necessary manpower and financial resources.

Implementation of Compliance Frameworks

Creating a detailed and effective compliance framework that covers data protection, ethical AI use and IP is challenging. Institutions must balance the need for innovation with regulatory requirements, ensuring that the framework evolves alongside new developments in AI and law. Implementing clear reporting mechanisms for compliance breaches and responding to incidents effectively requires strong institutional governance. Failure to act quickly on compliance issues could result in legal liabilities and damage to the institution's reputation.

The key challenges in regulatory compliance for AI adoption in legal education stem from the rapidly changing legal landscape, data privacy concerns, ethical dilemmas, IP complexities, resource limitations and the need for robust compliance frameworks. Institutions must stay proactive, adaptable and well resourced to manage these multiple challenges. Regulatory compliance in AI adoption for legal education is an ongoing and complex endeavour. Legal education institutions must invest in continuous regulatory awareness, engage with legal experts and establish robust compliance frameworks to ensure that AI initiatives align with both legal standards and ethical values. These efforts not only protect student data and IP but also contribute to the sustainability and ethical integrity of AI initiatives in legal education. By addressing these challenges proactively, institutions can navigate the evolving regulatory landscape and ensure the long-term success of AI-driven legal education.

6 Data Privacy and Security

Data privacy and security play a crucial role in AI-driven legal education due to the highly sensitive nature of legal information and the immense risks associated with potential data breaches. With AI being increasingly integrated into legal education, the safeguarding of sensitive data – including case records, client information and student data – becomes paramount. This presents sustainability challenges, particularly in balancing the protection of this information with fulfilment of educational and research goals. The risk of data breaches and unauthorised access to sensitive information is a significant concern that goes beyond legal education.[1] Universities often store and manage vast amounts of confidential data, making them prime targets for cyberattacks. AI systems used in legal education may inadvertently heighten this risk by introducing vulnerabilities through complex algorithms, vast data storage requirements or interconnected systems. In addition, the need for AI applications to access large datasets for training purposes brings questions around the ownership, ethical use and management of this data. Legal education institutions must therefore navigate various regulatory, legal and ethical considerations. The regulatory landscape for data protection is increasingly complex. Depending on the jurisdiction, universities must comply with strict regulations such as the GDPR in Europe or the CCPA in the United States. Ensuring ongoing compliance can be resource intensive, as it requires consistent monitoring, updating policies and possibly engaging experts to conduct audits. Furthermore, with students and legal professionals handling sensitive data regularly, ensuring that AI systems comply with these regulations is an ongoing and often costly challenge. Privacy-preserving technologies such as encryption, anonymisation and differential privacy are essential, but their implementation often requires sophisticated expertise and significant investment.

1 W. Luo, H. He, J. Liu, I. R. Berson, M. J. Berson, Y. Zhou and H. Li, 'Aladdin's Genie or Pandora's Box for Early Childhood Education? Experts Chat on the Roles, Challenges, and Developments of ChatGPT' (2023) *Early Education and Development* 1.

DOI: 10.4324/9781003607397-7

Sustainability challenges related to data privacy and security in AI-driven legal education involve striking a delicate balance between protecting sensitive data and fulfilling educational goals. AI applications in legal education depend on extensive data to function effectively and universities must determine who owns this data, especially when it includes sensitive or proprietary information. Navigating complex ethical frameworks concerning data ownership and responsible usage is a challenge, and institutions must ensure that AI models respect privacy and avoid discrimination. Institutions must ensure strict adherence to relevant regulations such as GDPR, CCPA or other local data protection laws. Compliance involves continuous monitoring, updating privacy policies and appointing designated officers, such as a data protection officer (DPO). Staying compliant while incorporating AI systems – many of which process personal and sensitive data – adds layers of complexity to data management practices. In AI-driven legal education, access to real-world data is critical for educational purposes, such as training students on practical cases. Balancing this need with data privacy concerns requires nuanced solutions like anonymising or pseudonymising sensitive information before using it in educational contexts. Institutions must consider carefully how much data to expose to students while maintaining the confidentiality of sensitive legal details. Balancing the need for privacy with educational goals is therefore a continual challenge. The following are key strategies for achieving this balance.

6.1 Establishing Robust Data Protection Policies and Practices

Institutions must adhere diligently to relevant data protection regulations, such as the GDPR.[2] Universities should also implement and continuously update their own data protection policies, appointing a DPO if necessary. Institutions must develop clear guidelines for handling sensitive legal information, ensuring that all staff and students understand the rules surrounding data protection and ethical handling. Regular audits of these policies are critical, with a focus on categorising data according to its sensitivity and adjusting retention practices to minimise unnecessary risk. Establishing clear data retention policies is vital to avoid stockpiling unnecessary data. Minimising the amount of data stored can help mitigate risks, as sensitive information will only be kept for the period necessary to meet educational objectives. AI-driven legal education systems should incorporate privacy-preserving technologies such as encryption, differential privacy and data anonymisation to protect sensitive information. These tools can reduce the risk of data breaches while allowing the systems to perform efficiently. In the context of legal education, the protection

---

2 EUR-Lex, 'Regulation (EU) 2016/679' (2016) <http://data.europa.eu/eli/reg/2016/679>.

of sensitive data is paramount, particularly as institutions increasingly adopt AI-driven technologies. Robust data protection policies must be established and continuously updated to meet evolving legal and ethical standards. To ensure compliance and mitigate risk, institutions should adopt a proactive approach, integrating data protection regulations such as the GDPR, CCPA and other relevant laws into their data management strategies.

6.1.1 Adherence to Regulatory Requirements

Legal education institutions must demonstrate strict compliance with data protection regulations. The GDPR, for example, mandates that any personal data collected and processed must adhere to key principles such as lawfulness, transparency, purpose limitation, data minimisation, accuracy and accountability. Institutions within or collaborating with organisations in the EU must comply with GDPR's stringent standards, such as obtaining explicit consent from individuals before collecting personal data, ensuring data subject rights like access and erasure, and maintaining robust data security measures. For institutions with international reach, it is essential to account for diverse privacy laws across jurisdictions. This requires collaboration between legal teams, compliance officers and IT departments to maintain compliance with various regulations globally.

6.1.2 Institutional Data Protection Policies

Beyond compliance with external regulations, universities must develop and maintain their own internal data protection policies, reflecting institutional values and operational needs. This includes ensuring that all stakeholders – including staff, students and faculty – understand and adhere to these policies. A DPO should be appointed, where necessary, to oversee data protection strategies and ensure compliance with regulations. This officer should be responsible for monitoring data protection activities, conducting regular audits and serving as a point of contact for data-related issues. Regular training sessions should be provided for faculty, staff and students on data protection principles, the ethical handling of sensitive legal information and how to apply these policies in daily academic and administrative activities. Faculty should be made aware of the specific regulations governing data in the legal education context, including how AI systems process and handle sensitive information.

6.1.3 Categorisation of Data Sensitivity

Institutions should adopt a data classification system that categorises information based on its sensitivity and risk. This approach enables the implementation of appropriate protections for each data category, mitigating the risk of exposure or misuse. Sensitive data – such as personally identifiable information

(PII), student records, legal case materials and faculty research – should be classified as high-risk and require stronger security measures, such as encryption and multi-factor authentication. Only authorised personnel should have access to sensitive data, with role-based access control (RBAC) limiting exposure to those with a legitimate need. Ensuring that access to sensitive legal data is restricted will help prevent breaches and misuse.

6.1.4 Data Retention and Minimisation Policies

A critical component of any robust data protection strategy is the implementation of data retention policies. Institutions should establish clear guidelines outlining how long different types of data are retained and when they should be deleted. Data should only be stored for the period necessary to achieve the intended purpose, after which it should be securely deleted. For example, legal education institutions may retain student performance data only for the duration required by academic programmes or accreditation purposes. The principle of data minimisation requires that institutions limit the collection and storage of personal data to what is strictly necessary. Reducing the amount of stored data reduces the risk of breaches and ensures compliance with data protection laws. Audits should be conducted to assess compliance with data retention policies, identifying outdated or unnecessary data that can be safely deleted. This helps to mitigate risk by preventing the accumulation of data that could be compromised in the event of a breach.

6.1.5 Use of Privacy-Preserving Technologies

To further protect sensitive information, AI-driven legal education systems should incorporate privacy-preserving technologies that enhance data security without compromising system functionality. Data encryption should be implemented across all storage and transmission points to protect sensitive information from unauthorised access. This is particularly important for legal data that may involve confidential case details or PII. By adding noise to data or otherwise anonymising it, differential privacy techniques ensure that AI systems can derive insights from large datasets without exposing individual information. This reduces the risk of re-identification in anonymised datasets. Where possible, data should be anonymised or pseudonymised to protect individuals' identities. This involves removing PII and replacing it with non-identifying markers, which can be reconnected to the original data only under strict conditions.

6.1.6 Continuous Monitoring and Incident Response

A key aspect of any data protection strategy is the establishment of continuous monitoring mechanisms and a well-defined incident response plan. These measures ensure that any potential breach is swiftly identified and addressed.

Institutions should deploy real-time monitoring tools that automatically scan for potential vulnerabilities or suspicious activities within the AI systems or databases. This proactive approach can help detect data breaches early and mitigate their impact. Institutions must develop a comprehensive incident response plan to address data breaches or leaks. The plan should include a clear chain of command, protocols for notifying affected individuals and steps for remediating the breach to prevent future occurrences.

6.1.7 Ethical Considerations and Compliance Audits

In addition to meeting regulatory requirements, data protection policies should reflect ethical considerations related to AI use in legal education. Institutions must ensure that AI systems are designed and implemented in ways that respect individuals' privacy rights. Regular ethical audits should be conducted to evaluate whether AI-driven educational tools are collecting and processing data in line with ethical principles such as informed consent, fairness and accountability. This includes assessing whether AI models are inadvertently discriminating against or unfairly affecting certain groups of students based on how data is used. Institutions should also perform legal compliance audits that assess adherence to data protection laws, reviewing areas such as data collection methods, processing activities, retention practices and third-party data sharing. These audits provide valuable insights into areas where compliance can be strengthened.

6.1.8 Institutional Oversight and Collaboration

Data protection is a collective responsibility, and institutions should foster a culture of collaboration between departments to ensure compliance with data protection standards. This includes establishing cross-departmental working groups that involve IT, legal, academic and administrative staff in data protection efforts. Collaboration between IT departments, legal teams and academic leadership ensures that all stakeholders are aligned in their approach to data protection. This collaborative approach allows for a more cohesive and effective implementation of data protection practices. Faculty, students and staff should be engaged regularly in discussions about data protection and privacy. This includes providing forums for stakeholders to voice concerns, ask questions and receive updates on changes to institutional policies.

Establishing robust data protection policies and practices is vital to ensure that AI-driven legal education systems adhere to both legal and ethical standards. By implementing comprehensive data protection policies, conducting regular audits, leveraging privacy-preserving technologies and fostering collaboration between departments, institutions can safeguard sensitive information, maintain compliance with regulations and mitigate risks associated with data breaches or misuse. Data protection efforts should be continuously updated and adapted to the evolving legal and technological landscape, ensuring that institutions remain at the forefront of responsible AI adoption.

6.2 Conducting Regular Security Audits and Vulnerability Assessments

Regular security audits and vulnerability assessments should be conducted by cybersecurity experts to identify weaknesses in AI systems and IT infrastructure. Penetration testing can simulate potential cyberattacks to evaluate an institution's preparedness and highlight areas needing improvement. Given that many vulnerabilities stem from unpatched systems, universities should maintain a rigorous patch management process to ensure that all software is regularly updated with the latest security fixes. Quick response times to any identified vulnerabilities are essential to preventing exploitation by malicious actors. Implementing strict user access controls can limit who has access to sensitive information, ensuring that only authorised individuals can view, process or modify the data. Continuous monitoring systems should track who accesses the data and how it is used, with detailed logs providing insight into potential security breaches. To maintain the integrity and security of AI systems and IT infrastructure in legal education, institutions must prioritise regular security audits and vulnerability assessments. These proactive measures help to identify and address weaknesses before they can be exploited by malicious actors. As legal education increasingly relies on AI and digital tools, ensuring robust cybersecurity practices is essential to protect sensitive data, including student information, legal case materials and institutional records.

6.2.1 Comprehensive Security Audits

Regular security audits should be conducted by cybersecurity experts to thoroughly assess the security posture of AI systems, databases and networks within the institution. These audits serve as a critical review of existing security policies, practices and configurations, identifying vulnerabilities that could be exploited by attackers. Audits should encompass both internal evaluations of the institution's IT infrastructure and external penetration testing, where security experts simulate real-world cyberattacks. This dual approach provides a comprehensive view of potential vulnerabilities, from within the system and outside threats. Specific attention should be given to the security of AI systems, including how they collect, process and store data. AI algorithms, data pipelines and underlying infrastructure must be scrutinised for potential security gaps, as vulnerabilities in AI systems could lead to significant data breaches or manipulation of AI outputs. Audits should cover hardware, software, networks, data storage and user access controls. Special emphasis should be placed on cloud services and third-party applications used by the institution, as these can be significant sources of vulnerability.

6.2.2 Penetration Testing

Institutions should regularly conduct penetration testing (also known as ethical hacking) to simulate cyberattacks and assess the institution's preparedness to respond to potential threats. Penetration tests reveal how well existing security measures can withstand targeted attacks and highlight specific areas for improvement. Penetration testers simulate different types of cyberattacks – such as phishing, Structured Query Language (SQL) injection and ransomware attacks – to evaluate the effectiveness of the institution's defence mechanisms. These simulations help to identify weaknesses in the system's firewalls, encryption protocols and intrusion detection systems. Penetration testing should be designed to mimic real-world attack scenarios, including attacks targeting AI models, data leaks through application programming interface (API) vulnerabilities and unauthorised access to sensitive data stored in institutional servers. By using these scenarios, institutions can evaluate their incident response plans and cybersecurity protocols under realistic conditions. After testing, penetration testers provide a detailed report outlining the vulnerabilities identified and the severity of each weakness, along with recommended remediation actions. Institutions should prioritise fixing critical vulnerabilities first and develop mitigation plans for less severe issues.

6.2.3 Patch Management and Software Updates

Many cybersecurity vulnerabilities stem from outdated or unpatched software. Institutions must adopt a rigorous patch management process to ensure that all software and systems are updated regularly with the latest security patches and fixes. Establishing clear patch management policies ensures that updates are applied consistently and promptly across all systems. These policies should include protocols for monitoring software vendors for updates, conducting compatibility testing and automating patch deployment where possible. Prioritise the installation of patches that address critical vulnerabilities or high-risk security flaws. Delaying these updates can leave the institution exposed to attacks that could compromise AI systems, data integrity and overall network security. Using automated patch management tools can streamline the update process, ensuring that patches are applied in a timely manner without disrupting system operations. These tools also provide reports on patch compliance, allowing IT teams to verify that updates have been successfully deployed.

6.2.4 User Access Controls

Institutions should implement strict user access controls to limit who has the ability to access sensitive information and critical AI systems. By enforcing least-privilege access, institutions can minimise the risk of insider threats or unauthorised access to critical data. Implement RBAC that assigns users access privileges based on their roles and responsibilities. This ensures that only authorised personnel – such as faculty, IT staff or administrators – can access or modify sensitive data. Implementing multi-factor authentication (MFA) adds an extra layer of security by requiring users to provide two or more verification factors before gaining access. MFA can help prevent unauthorised access even if user credentials are compromised. For users who require access to highly sensitive systems or datasets, privileged access management (PAM) tools can be used to monitor and control their activities. PAM systems create audit trails, recording all actions taken by privileged users and flagging any suspicious behaviour.

6.2.5 Continuous Monitoring and Log Management

Institutions should implement continuous monitoring systems that track access to data, system activity and network traffic in real time. This allows cybersecurity teams to detect potential breaches or suspicious activity as it occurs. Real-time monitoring tools should be employed to continuously track who accesses the data, when they access it and how it is used. Monitoring systems should also include anomaly detection, flagging unusual activity that could indicate a security breach. Maintaining detailed logs of all user activities and system events is essential for investigating potential security incidents. These audit trails provide insight into who accessed sensitive data, what actions were taken and whether any unauthorised changes were made. In the event of a security breach, having an effective incident response plan in place is crucial. The plan should outline clear communication protocols, define roles and responsibilities, and specify steps for containment, investigation and remediation.

6.2.6 Third-Party Security Assessments

Many universities rely on third-party vendors for services such as cloud storage, AI tools and software applications. To ensure the security of these external services, institutions must conduct third-party security assessments and demand robust security measures from vendors. Institutions should conduct thorough risk assessments of third-party vendors before integrating their services. This includes evaluating the vendor's security policies, data protection measures and compliance with regulations such as GDPR and CCPA. Law schools can request regular third-party security audits to verify that vendors are maintaining high standards of cybersecurity. These audits should include reviews of data encryption, access controls and incident response protocols used by the vendor. Institutions should establish data sharing agreements that outline security requirements for vendors. These agreements should specify how data will be protected, who has access to it and the protocols in place for handling data breaches.

6.2.7 Security Awareness Training

A well-trained faculty and student body are essential for maintaining the institution's cybersecurity posture. Security awareness training should be provided to all staff, faculty and students to ensure they understand the risks associated with cyberthreats and how to prevent them. Training should focus on phishing attacks, which are a common method used by cybercriminals to gain access to systems. Faculty and students should be taught how to recognise suspicious emails and avoid clicking on malicious links. Law schools should emphasise the importance of strong passwords and the use of password managers to store and manage login credentials securely. Password policies should encourage frequent password changes and prohibit the use of weak passwords. Staff and students should be encouraged to report suspicious activity or potential security incidents immediately. Clear reporting channels should be established so that any potential threats can be investigated promptly.

Conducting regular security audits and vulnerability assessments is critical to safeguarding AI systems and IT infrastructure in legal education. By implementing penetration testing, maintaining a rigorous patch management process, enforcing strict user access controls and utilising continuous monitoring systems, institutions can identify and mitigate potential security threats. Regular training and third-party assessments further enhance the institution's cybersecurity posture, ensuring that faculty, staff and students are well equipped to protect sensitive data and maintain compliance with security standards.

6.3 Providing Training and Awareness Programmes

Training programmes focusing on cyberhygiene – such as recognising phishing attacks, maintaining strong password protocols and securely handling sensitive information – are critical. These should be mandatory for both staff and students, especially given the heightened risks associated with AI systems handling sensitive data in legal contexts. Training should extend beyond technical practices to include ethical considerations, instilling in future legal professionals a strong sense of responsibility around data privacy. Participants should also understand how to recognise and respond to potential security breaches, including knowing the importance of quick reporting when an issue is suspected. Universities must have an incident response plan in place to swiftly address data breaches when they occur. These plans should outline roles and responsibilities, communication strategies and the steps to mitigate the damage caused by breaches. In today's digital landscape, the proliferation of AI systems in legal education requires both staff and students to be well versed in cybersecurity and data protection practices. Training and awareness programmes are essential for safeguarding sensitive information, especially when AI tools are integrated into legal education. These programmes should cover not only technical skills but also ethical considerations, ensuring that participants are prepared to manage data responsibly and respond effectively to security threats.

6.3.1 Cyberhygiene Training

A foundational aspect of any security training programme is cyberhygiene – the daily practices and habits that keep digital environments secure. All participants, including faculty, students and administrative staff, must be trained in essential cybersecurity practices such as recognising phishing attacks, maintaining strong password protocols and secure handling of sensitive information. Phishing is one of the most common tactics used by cybercriminals to gain unauthorised access to systems. Training should teach participants how to spot phishing emails, links and other deceptive tactics designed to steal personal information or inject malware into a system. Real-world examples and phishing simulations can help individuals become more adept at identifying these threats. Password security is a crucial aspect of cyberhygiene. Training should emphasise the importance of creating strong, unique passwords and using MFA for added protection. Faculty and students should be encouraged to use password managers to store their credentials securely and reduce the risk of password-related breaches. Participants should be trained on how to handle sensitive data – including legal documents, student records and research materials – with utmost care. This includes secure file sharing, data encryption practices and guidelines on securely storing and transmitting sensitive information to prevent unauthorised access.

6.3.2 Mandatory Training for All Staff and Students

Given the heightened risks associated with AI systems handling sensitive legal data, it is essential that cybersecurity training is mandatory for all staff and students. Both groups interact with sensitive data on a regular basis, making them key stakeholders in ensuring its security. Institutions should implement mandatory annual training sessions to keep participants updated on the latest cybersecurity practices and emerging threats. This ensures that both new and returning members of the institution are consistently aware of best practices and can adapt to the evolving digital landscape. Different roles within the institution may require specific training. For instance, administrative staff managing large databases might need more intensive training on data encryption and access control, while faculty using AI tools in research or legal education would benefit from training on how to secure AI systems and mitigate biases in data handling.

6.3.3 Ethical Considerations and AI

In addition to technical training, it is critical to integrate ethical considerations into the curriculum, particularly in the context of AI. Future legal professionals must understand the broader implications of data privacy and responsible AI use. Legal professionals have a duty to protect client information and uphold data privacy laws, such as the GDPR. Training should focus on these responsibilities and educate students and staff on how to ensure compliance with data protection regulations in all AI-related activities. Participants should be made aware of the potential biases that can emerge in AI systems, particularly in legal settings. This includes understanding how AI algorithms are trained, how data biases can affect outcomes and the steps needed to ensure that AI systems are used ethically and responsibly in legal education and practice.

6.3.4 Incident Response Training

Beyond preventive measures, staff and students should be trained to recognise and respond to security breaches or suspicious activity. Understanding how to react quickly and effectively can limit the damage caused by breaches and minimise the risk of further compromise. Training should include education on how to identify potential security breaches or anomalies, such as unexpected system behaviour, unauthorised access or suspicious emails. Faculty and students should be aware of early warning signs, including notifications of unusual login attempts or unexplained changes in data access patterns. Quick reporting of potential security breaches is essential. Training should ensure that all participants understand the institution's incident reporting procedures and who to contact if they suspect a breach. Early reporting can enable IT teams to investigate and contain the issue before it escalates.

6.3.5 Incident Response Plans

Each university must have a clear incident response plan in place to swiftly and effectively address data breaches when they occur. This plan should outline the roles and responsibilities of each team member, the steps to take in response to a breach and strategies for damage control and mitigation. The incident response plan should clearly define who is responsible for handling different aspects of a security breach, from IT staff and legal teams to communication teams and faculty. Establishing a chain of command ensures that members of each team know their roles and can respond quickly. In the event of a breach, clear communication with all relevant stakeholders – including students, faculty and external partners – is critical. The response plan should include communication protocols to notify affected parties, reassure them of the steps being taken and provide guidance on what they need to do to protect themselves. Once a breach has been detected, the institution's priority is to contain and mitigate the damage. The response plan should include detailed steps for isolating compromised systems, conducting forensic investigations and rebuilding affected networks. Universities should also plan for public relations responses to minimise reputational damage and maintain trust.

6.3.6 Ongoing Education and Updates

Cybersecurity threats are constantly evolving, so training and awareness programmes must be updated regularly to reflect new threats, technological advancements and regulatory changes. Continuous learning should be encouraged through regular refreshers, workshops and webinars, and interactive simulations. Universities should offer quarterly or semi-annual refresher courses that provide updates on the latest security threats and best practices. This will help ensure that participants remain vigilant and well prepared for emerging cybersecurity challenges. Hosting cybersecurity workshops or webinars led by experts can provide additional insights and reinforce training. These sessions can cover specific topics like advanced phishing techniques, social engineering and AI-related vulnerabilities. Using interactive simulations such as phishing tests or breach response drills can help participants apply what they have learned in real-world scenarios. These exercises improve preparedness and confidence in handling potential security issues.

Implementing comprehensive training and awareness programmes is crucial for fostering a strong security culture in institutions that integrate AI into legal education. By ensuring all staff and students receive both technical and ethical training, universities can significantly reduce their risk of security breaches and ensure compliance with data protection regulations. Additionally, having robust incident response plans and ongoing education will enable institutions to remain agile and responsive in the face of evolving cybersecurity threats.

Practical Tips

Balancing data protection and educational goals in AI-driven legal education requires a proactive, multi-pronged approach. By implementing robust cybersecurity practices, complying with regulations and promoting ethical data usage, institutions can safeguard sensitive data while advancing their educational missions.

By adopting these comprehensive measures, legal education institutions can build a strong foundation for data privacy and security in the era of AI-driven education. Such proactive efforts not only protect sensitive information but also instil a culture of responsibility and awareness among students, faculty and staff, ultimately enhancing the institution's overall cybersecurity posture. The strategies outlined in this section for addressing data privacy and security in AI-driven legal education present several challenges that institutions may encounter.

Complexity in Data Ownership and Ethical Use

Determining who owns the data – especially when it comes to sensitive or proprietary information – can be difficult. Legal education institutions may face challenges in navigating the legal and ethical frameworks governing data collection, usage and sharing. This becomes even more complex when using data from multiple jurisdictions or handling cross-border data, each with different regulations. Implementing privacy-preserving technologies like encryption or anonymisation can be technically complex and require significant investment in infrastructure and expertise.

Ongoing Regulatory Compliance

Keeping up with evolving regulations, such as the GDPR or CCPA, can be resource intensive, as regulations often change and institutions must adapt continually. Ensuring compliance with multiple – sometimes conflicting – data protection laws across jurisdictions can complicate data handling procedures, especially in international educational settings. Continuous updates to policies, regular audits and compliance with intricate regulatory frameworks can require dedicated staff and financial resources, making it challenging for institutions with limited budgets.

Resource and Cost Constraints

Many of the proposed strategies, including security audits, vulnerability assessments and the adoption of privacy-preserving technologies, can be costly. Universities often operate under tight budgets and allocating sufficient resources to these areas may be challenging. Additionally, the constant need for software updates and security patches can strain IT departments. Funding for these initiatives can be limited, particularly for smaller institutions, making it hard to ensure ongoing compliance and security without sacrificing other areas of academic development.

Technological and Operational Challenges

Implementing and managing privacy-preserving technologies (like anonymisation or differential privacy) can be technically complex and might require specialised expertise that many institutions lack. Maintaining the delicate balance between privacy and educational goals can also lead to operational inefficiencies, where overly strict data policies hinder access to useful data for teaching and research. Deploying these tools often requires significant upfront investments in hardware, software and staff training. Even with the right tools, applying these technologies across the board consistently can be challenging.

Cultural and Educational Barriers

Promoting a culture of awareness of data privacy and security matters requires continuous training, awareness programmes and a shift in mindset across students, staff and faculty. Legal education institutions may face resistance from individuals who are accustomed to traditional data management practices or unaware of the severity of potential cyberthreats. It can be difficult to maintain engagement in security awareness programmes and ensure that the training is effective. Additionally, the constantly evolving nature of cyberthreats requires regular updates to training programmes, which can be time consuming and resource intensive.

Balancing Educational Needs With Privacy Needs

AI systems need large datasets for proper functioning, but the sensitive nature of legal data raises concerns about exposing confidential information to students or AI algorithms. Ensuring that educational goals are met without compromising privacy can create tension between access to necessary data and the need for strict confidentiality. The tension between data access for educational purposes and maintaining privacy could hinder teaching and research initiatives, especially if AI systems are over-restricted due to privacy concerns.

Incident Response and Data Breach Management

Despite strong preventive measures, data breaches are still a possibility, and institutions may not always be fully prepared to respond. Legal education institutions must develop, communicate and regularly test their incident response plans, which can be challenging given the need for speed and coordination in the event of a breach. Simulated exercises and incident response planning can be resource heavy, requiring coordinated efforts across departments, which may slow down the implementation or improvement of incident response strategies.

User Access Control and Monitoring

Implementing and maintaining strict access control protocols and continuous monitoring of data usage can lead to operational inefficiencies. Users may experience reduced access to necessary information, or there may be delays in retrieving data due to heightened security measures. Managing and balancing user permissions for large institutions with many stakeholders (students, faculty, researchers, administrators) can be cumbersome and require advanced access management systems.

Legal education institutions face numerous challenges in maintaining data privacy and security in AI-driven education. These include complexities in data ownership, regulatory compliance, financial and resource constraints, technological difficulties, cultural barriers and operational inefficiencies. Navigating these challenges successfully requires a proactive, well-resourced and multi-faceted approach that balances security needs with educational goals. Balancing data privacy with the educational imperatives of AI-driven legal education requires a range of strategies that include regulatory compliance, robust data protection policies, continuous training and privacy-preserving technologies. Institutions must adopt a proactive stance, regularly updating their data management practices and cybersecurity measures. By building a solid foundation of data privacy and security, universities can safeguard sensitive legal information while embracing the transformative potential of AI in legal education. These measures not only protect the institution but also help foster a culture of responsibility, ensuring students and staff understand the critical role they play in maintaining data security.

7 Long-Term Viability of AI Solutions

Sustainability also involves considering the long-term viability of AI solutions in legal education. Institutions must assess the sustainability of their AI investments and ensure that the benefits continue to outweigh the costs over time. For instance, uncertainty can affect user perceptions and interactions with AI.[1] In the context of legal education, therefore, ensuring a positive user experience and engagement with AI-driven educational tools is crucial for their effective adoption and long-term sustainability. Smith highlights the importance of educators adapting to technological advancements.[2] This adaptability is relevant when addressing the evolving nature of AI and ensuring that legal education keeps pace with AI developments. Ensuring the long-term viability of AI solutions in legal education is a dynamic process that requires careful planning, continuous evaluation and adaptability. Changes in technology and educational needs can affect the sustainability of AI solutions in legal education significantly, and rapid advancements in AI technology may render existing solutions obsolete. Institutions must stay abreast of these changes and update their AI infrastructure and strategies accordingly. As legal education evolves, the needs of students and faculty may change. AI solutions should align with these evolving needs, whether in terms of content delivery, assessment methods or research support. Changes in educational pedagogy may require adjustments to AI solutions. For example, shifts toward experiential learning or competency-based education may necessitate different AI tools and resources. Evolving regulations related to data privacy, IP or ethical considerations may affect the use of AI in legal education, and institutions must ensure that AI initiatives remain compliant.

The sustainability of AI solutions in legal education is a dynamic and ongoing process that requires careful planning, evaluation and adaptability.

---

1 S. Pan, J. Cui and Y. Mou, 'Desirable or Distasteful? Exploring Uncertainty in Human-Chatbot Relationships' (2023) *International Journal of Human – Computer Interaction* 1.
2 M. Smith, 'Integrating Technology in Contemporary Legal Education' (2020) 54 *The Law Teacher* 209.

DOI: 10.4324/9781003607397-8

Changes in technology, education and regulation will significantly affect the long-term effectiveness of AI solutions. Institutions must evaluate their AI infrastructure continuously and make adjustments to remain at the forefront of technological advancements while ensuring that AI solutions align with their educational mission. To address this aspect of sustainability effectively, institutions should consider the following strategies.

7.1 Continuous Cost–Benefit Evaluation

The fast-paced nature of AI technology means that solutions implemented today may become outdated in a relatively short time. As AI algorithms, hardware and software evolve, institutions must be proactive in updating or replacing older systems. This constant need for upgrades poses a significant challenge to the long-term viability of AI in legal education, as it requires sustained investment in new technology and training for educators and staff. To address this, institutions should stay updated on AI trends, collaborate with AI vendors to access cutting-edge technologies and build long-term partnerships that allow for smoother transitions to new systems. Periodic reviews of the institution's AI infrastructure ensure that it remains relevant and aligned with the latest advancements. Conducting a comprehensive analysis of the costs associated with AI implementations throughout their lifecycle should include initial investment, maintenance, upgrades and eventual retirement. These costs can be compared to the benefits derived from AI, including improved educational outcomes, resource optimisation and operational efficiency. Institutions can calculate the return on investment of AI solutions by quantifying both the tangible and intangible returns over time. Tangible returns may include cost savings, while intangible returns may encompass enhanced student engagement and learning experiences. Regularly benchmarking the performance and cost-effectiveness of AI solutions against industry standards and peer institutions helps identify areas for improvement and ensures that AI initiatives remain competitive and sustainable.

As the rapid advancement of AI technology continues to reshape the landscape of legal education, institutions must regularly assess the effectiveness and sustainability of their AI implementations. Continuous cost–benefit evaluation is vital to ensure that AI systems remain cost-effective, relevant and aligned with institutional goals over time. This process involves not only assessing the financial implications of AI adoption but also evaluating the educational benefits, operational efficiency and long-term viability of these technologies.

7.1.1 Keeping Up With Evolving AI Technologies

AI technologies – including algorithms, hardware and software – evolve at a fast pace. Solutions that are on the cutting edge today may become obsolete within a short period of time, necessitating a proactive approach to maintaining up-to-date systems. Institutions must assess their AI infrastructure regularly to avoid falling behind and ensure that students and faculty are working with the most relevant technologies available. Institutions should monitor AI advancements and industry trends continuously to stay informed about emerging technologies and innovations. This includes developments in ML, NLP and other AI subfields that affect legal education. Staying informed enables universities to make timely decisions about upgrading or replacing outdated AI systems. Partnerships with AI vendors can provide early access to cutting-edge technologies and updates. By building long-term relationships with trusted vendors, institutions can ensure smoother transitions when updating systems or adopting new technologies. Vendor collaborations may also include training programmes, helping educators and staff remain proficient in the latest AI tools. Establishing partnerships with AI research institutions, technology firms and legal tech companies can enhance access to state-of-the-art AI tools and frameworks. These collaborations foster innovation and enable universities to align their AI strategies with industry standards, helping them stay competitive.

7.1.2 Periodic Reviews of AI Infrastructure

Conducting regular reviews of AI infrastructure is essential to ensure that systems remain aligned with current technology standards and the institution's educational objectives. These reviews should encompass the performance, cost-effectiveness and long-term viability of AI implementation, identifying potential gaps or inefficiencies. Periodic evaluations should assess how well AI systems perform in terms of accuracy, efficiency and usability. This includes reviewing the effectiveness of AI-driven learning platforms, automated grading systems and legal research tools. Regular performance benchmarks ensure that AI systems continue to meet the needs of students and faculty. AI tools should remain aligned with institutional goals and responsive to the evolving demands of legal education. By reviewing whether AI applications are still relevant and valuable, institutions can determine if they should be updated, upgraded or replaced. Outdated or inefficient systems that no longer contribute to positive outcomes may be retired in favour of newer technologies.

7.1.3 Comprehensive Cost Analysis

AI adoption comes with both upfront and ongoing costs, including hardware investments, software licences and training for educators and staff. Conducting a comprehensive cost analysis helps institutions better understand the financial implications of AI adoption throughout its lifecycle. The initial cost of acquiring AI technologies – such as purchasing hardware, software licences or third-party AI services – must be considered carefully. Institutions should weigh these costs against the expected educational and operational benefits of AI implementation. AI systems require ongoing maintenance to ensure smooth operation and upgrades to keep pace with technological advances. Regular system updates, software patches and hardware replacements are critical for maintaining AI efficiency, but they also add to long-term operational costs. As AI technologies become obsolete, institutions must account for the costs associated with retiring outdated systems. This may involve decommissioning servers, disposing of old hardware or migrating data to newer platforms. Proper planning for retirement costs helps avoid financial surprises later in the technology's lifecycle.

7.1.4 Calculating Return on Investment

A thorough cost–benefit analysis should calculate the return on investment (ROI) for AI solutions, taking both tangible and intangible returns into account. This helps institutions understand whether the benefits of AI adoption justify the financial investment. Tangible returns can include cost savings from automating administrative tasks, improving operational efficiency or reducing the need for human intervention in certain processes. For example, AI-driven grading systems or legal research platforms can reduce manual workload significantly, leading to measurable time and cost savings. While harder to quantify, intangible returns are equally important. These may include enhanced student engagement, improved learning outcomes and more personalised educational experiences. AI's ability to adapt content to individual learners' needs can foster more effective learning and increased student satisfaction, which may contribute to better retention rates and academic success. AI's role in improving teaching quality and student success should be factored into ROI calculations. For example, AI tools that offer adaptive learning experiences, simulate real-world legal scenarios or provide instant feedback can enhance the learning process and contribute to better overall academic performance.

7.1.5 Benchmarking and Peer Comparisons

Regularly benchmarking the institution's AI initiatives against industry standards and peer institutions provides insights into areas for improvement and innovation. Institutions can compare cost-effectiveness, performance and impact to ensure that their AI strategies remain competitive and sustainable. Engaging in peer comparisons can reveal whether an institution is ahead, on par or falling behind in its use of AI. For example, universities can compare the quality of their AI-driven learning platforms, their investment levels and the outcomes achieved. This can inform decisions on where to focus future resources or improvements. Keeping an eye on industry standards for AI in education ensures that institutions are following best practices and benefiting from proven methodologies. This can help identify inefficiencies in AI systems or highlight areas where further investment or upgrades may be required to stay at the forefront of legal education technology.

7.1.6 Sustainability and Long-Term Viability

As AI technologies continue to evolve, institutions must consider the long-term sustainability of their AI strategies. Regular cost–benefit evaluations ensure that AI initiatives not only meet current needs but are also scalable and adaptable for future growth. Institutions must be prepared for ongoing investments in AI technologies. This includes budgeting for regular upgrades, maintenance and training programmes that keep staff and students up to date with the latest tools and best practices. Sustained investment ensures that AI systems continue to deliver value over the long term. Adopting technologies that are scalable and modular allows institutions to adapt to new advancements without overhauling entire systems. This reduces the risk of obsolescence and ensures that AI platforms remain useful as the field of AI and legal education evolves.

Continuous cost–benefit evaluation is critical to the successful integration of AI in legal education. By staying proactive in tracking AI trends, collaborating with external vendors and conducting regular reviews, institutions can ensure their AI systems remain relevant and effective. A comprehensive analysis of costs, benefits and ROI ensures that AI initiatives are sustainable over the long term, providing both tangible and intangible returns that justify ongoing investment. Through benchmarking, regular updates and future-proofing efforts, universities can ensure that their AI strategies contribute to the continuous improvement of legal education.

7.2 Scalability and Adaptability

As legal education evolves, so too do the needs of students and educators. AI solutions must adapt to changes in educational pedagogy, such as the shift toward experiential learning, competency-based education or online learning environments. These shifts may require the use of different AI tools, including virtual simulations, AI-driven tutoring systems or AI-based assessments that align with these new approaches. AI tools must be scalable and flexible to adapt to these shifts. Institutions should continually engage faculty and students to assess their needs and ensure that the AI solutions implemented reflect the evolving demands of legal education. Before adopting AI solutions, assessing their scalability to accommodate fluctuations in enrolment, evolving curricula and emerging educational trends ensures that AI initiatives can grow and adapt to meet changing needs. Recognising that AI technologies evolve rapidly and implementing solutions that are adaptable to changing technological landscapes avoids obsolescence and ensures long-term relevance. Investing in modular, cloud-based or open-source AI solutions that allow for continuous improvement and expansion as needed ensures that AI systems remain relevant in the face of changing educational needs.

In the context of legal education, scalability and adaptability are critical for ensuring that AI solutions remain relevant and effective over time. As both education and technology continue to evolve, AI systems must be designed to handle changes in student demographics, teaching methods and institutional needs without becoming obsolete. By focusing on scalability and adaptability, legal education institutions can future-proof their AI investments, ensuring that they can accommodate shifting educational trends, new pedagogies and technological advancements.

7.2.1 Adapting to Changing Educational Pedagogy

Legal education is increasingly moving beyond traditional lecture-based learning toward more innovative and student-centred approaches. AI systems need to adapt to new pedagogical shifts, such as experiential learning, competency-based education and online and hybrid learning. The rise of hands-on learning methods – such as simulations, internships and clinic-based experiences – requires AI tools that can simulate real-world legal environments. AI-driven virtual simulations can help students practice legal procedures, interact with clients and engage in courtroom simulations, providing an immersive learning experience. This model emphasises mastery of specific skills and competencies rather than seat time. AI-powered adaptive learning systems can personalise educational content, track students' progress and provide customised feedback based on their individual learning needs and pace. This flexibility ensures that each student develops the necessary skills for legal practice at their own speed. With the increased adoption of online learning platforms, AI tools must integrate seamlessly into both fully remote and blended learning environments. This includes AI-based assessments, virtual classrooms and AI-driven tutoring systems that help students access resources anytime, anywhere. These tools must scale effectively to support large, diverse student populations and adapt to different delivery methods.

7.2.2 Scalability for Growing Enrolments and Curriculum Changes

The scalability of AI systems is essential for accommodating fluctuations in student enrolment, evolving curricula and the growing complexity of legal education. Key considerations include fluctuating enrolment, evolving curricula and emerging trends in legal education. As enrolment numbers fluctuate, particularly with the rise of online programmes that attract global students, AI systems must be capable of supporting large volumes of students without compromising performance. Scalable AI infrastructure allows institutions to handle increasing student numbers by adjusting resource allocation automatically, ensuring consistent user experience for all students. As the legal profession evolves, so does the curriculum in law schools. New courses and specialisations may require the integration of different AI tools, such as those that focus on areas like legal technology, data privacy and AI ethics. Institutions need AI systems that are flexible and can be reconfigured easily to align with new course content, faculty teaching styles and student needs. Legal education is constantly shaped by global trends such as changes in regulatory frameworks, technological advancements and the increasing use of legal tech in practice. AI systems must be designed with the ability to incorporate new tools, datasets and methodologies to remain in line with these trends. For instance, if there is a shift toward AI-based legal research tools, the institution's AI infrastructure must be capable of integrating these new technologies seamlessly.

7.2.3 Engaging Faculty and Students in Continuous Assessment

Ongoing engagement with faculty and students is essential for assessing the effectiveness of AI solutions and ensuring that they continue to meet the evolving demands of legal education. This continuous feedback loop allows institutions to fine-tune their AI systems to ensure relevance, flexibility and user satisfaction. Faculty play a critical role in identifying areas where AI tools can enhance teaching, learning and administrative tasks. Regular input from faculty on how well AI tools align with their teaching methods and curricula ensures that AI initiatives support educational goals. By involving faculty in the selection and development of AI systems, institutions can implement solutions that address real classroom challenges and pedagogical needs. Students are the primary beneficiaries of AI-driven education, making their feedback essential in evaluating the impact of AI tools on their learning experiences. By conducting regular surveys, focus groups and pilot testing, institutions can gather valuable insights on the usability, effectiveness and scalability of AI solutions. Student feedback can also highlight any gaps in the current AI infrastructure that may need to be addressed to meet the growing needs of diverse student populations.

7.2.4 Investing in Modular and Cloud-Based AI Solutions

To ensure scalability and adaptability, legal education institutions should invest in modular, cloud-based or open-source AI solutions that allow for continuous improvement and expansion as needed. These types of systems provide significant advantages in terms of flexibility and long-term viability. Modular AI solutions consist of interchangeable components that can be upgraded or replaced easily without overhauling the entire system. This enables institutions to implement new features, tools or functionalities as needed, ensuring that the system can adapt to changes in pedagogy, enrolment or technology. For example, an institution may add an AI-based legal writing tool to its existing AI infrastructure without disrupting other aspects of the system. Cloud-based AI platforms offer scalability on demand, making them ideal for institutions experiencing fluctuating enrolment numbers or expanding their online programmes. Cloud systems allow for flexible resource allocation, enabling institutions to scale up or down depending on the number of users, courses or programmes being supported. Cloud-based solutions also ensure that AI tools are accessible from any location, enhancing the adaptability of online learning. Open-source AI technologies provide a cost-effective and customisable option for institutions looking to implement scalable AI systems. These solutions allow institutions to build and adapt AI tools to meet specific educational needs, fostering innovation and continuous improvement. Open-source AI also encourages collaboration with other institutions and developers, leading to the creation of shared resources and best practices.

7.2.5 Ensuring Adaptability to Rapid Technological Change

AI technologies evolve rapidly, making adaptability a critical factor in ensuring long-term success. Institutions must consider the future growth of AI systems, ensuring that they are designed to accommodate emerging technological landscapes and avoid becoming obsolete. Institutions should adopt AI solutions that are adaptable to future advancements, such as improvements in NLP, ML and predictive analytics. Future-proof AI systems are built with scalability in mind, enabling institutions to integrate new tools, datasets or methodologies as they emerge without needing to overhaul existing infrastructure. Staying abreast of emerging technologies such as quantum computing, edge AI or fifth-generation cellular network (5G) connectivity allows institutions to explore innovative ways to enhance their AI systems. By continuously evaluating the potential of these technologies to affect legal education, institutions can remain at the forefront of AI-driven learning and ensure that their systems are adaptable to technological shifts.

7.2.6 Minimising Obsolescence and Ensuring Long-Term Relevance

AI systems must be designed with longevity in mind to avoid the high costs associated with frequent replacements or upgrades. Institutions can minimise the risk of obsolescence by adopting scalable and adaptable AI technologies that remain relevant as legal education evolves. Regular updates to AI systems – such as implementing new software patches, upgrading hardware or incorporating the latest AI algorithms – help ensure that the system remains efficient and relevant. Institutions should work closely with AI vendors to ensure that their systems receive the necessary updates to maintain optimal performance over time. Institutions should avoid becoming locked into proprietary AI systems that are difficult or costly to update. By opting for open standards or interoperable AI systems, institutions can ensure greater flexibility in incorporating new tools or transitioning to new technologies when needed.

In the rapidly evolving landscape of legal education, scalability and adaptability are essential for the successful implementation and sustainability of AI solutions. By focusing on these principles, institutions can ensure that their AI systems remain relevant, flexible and capable of meeting the changing needs of both educators and students. Investing in modular, cloud-based or open-source AI solutions allows institutions to scale their AI initiatives in line with technological advances and pedagogical shifts. Engaging faculty and students in continuous assessment ensures that AI solutions remain aligned with educational goals and user needs, while future-proofing strategies help minimise obsolescence and maintain long-term relevance. Through careful planning and regular evaluation, legal education institutions can create adaptable, scalable AI systems that support their mission in the years to come.

7.3 Strategic Updates

Legal education institutions must comply with a wide range of regulations, especially concerning data privacy, IP and ethical use of AI. As governments and regulatory bodies introduce new rules for AI, institutions must ensure that their AI-driven solutions remain compliant. Failure to do so can lead to legal challenges and ethical concerns. Institutions should establish dedicated legal and compliance teams to monitor regulatory changes, develop robust compliance frameworks, and work with AI vendors to ensure adherence to the latest guidelines. Legal compliance should be considered from the design phase of AI tools to avoid costly retroactive modifications. Institutions must develop and maintain a dynamic AI strategy that reflects changing technologies and educational needs, periodically reviewing and updating this strategy to align with institutional goals and respond to emerging trends. Creating technological roadmaps, which outline the anticipated evolution of AI solutions and their integration into legal education, provides a forward-looking perspective for long-term planning. Fostering a culture of innovation within the institution, encouraging faculty and staff to propose new AI applications and improvements to existing ones, ensures that AI remains at the forefront of educational practices.

In the rapidly evolving landscape of AI in legal education, institutions must be proactive in managing the intersection of technology, regulation and pedagogy. Strategic updates are essential to ensure that AI-driven solutions remain compliant with emerging regulations, address ethical concerns and align with the institution's long-term goals. Regularly updating AI strategies, compliance frameworks and technology roadmaps ensures that legal education institutions can navigate the complex legal and technological environment with confidence.

7.3.1 Staying Ahead of Regulatory Changes

Legal education institutions are subject to a wide array of regulations, particularly around data privacy, IP and the ethical use of AI. As governments and regulatory bodies continue to refine their policies on AI, staying updated on these changes is critical to avoiding legal challenges and maintaining ethical AI practices. Compliance with data privacy laws such as the GDPR and CCPA is non-negotiable, as legal education institutions often handle sensitive student data. With AI systems processing large amounts of personal information, it is important to ensure that data privacy protocols are up to date. Institutions should monitor regulatory updates and adjust their data protection measures to reflect new legal requirements. AI tools used in legal education may involve the use of proprietary software, research data and educational content. Ensuring that IP rights are respected, especially when integrating third-party AI solutions, helps avoid potential legal disputes. Regular reviews of licensing agreements, copyright policies and data usage contracts ensure that institutions remain in compliance with IP laws. Beyond legal compliance, AI use in legal education must adhere to ethical standards. Institutions should follow established AI ethics guidelines, such as those developed by the Institute of Electrical and Electronics Engineers (IEEE), OECD or other AI governance bodies. Ethical considerations surrounding bias, fairness and transparency in AI must be central to the development and deployment of AI tools.

7.3.2 Establishing Dedicated Legal and Compliance Teams

Institutions should establish dedicated legal and compliance teams responsible for monitoring changes in AI-related regulations and ensuring adherence to the latest standards. These teams should work in tandem with AI vendors, faculty and IT departments to develop robust compliance frameworks, collaborate with AI vendors and incorporate legal compliance in the design phase. Creating comprehensive compliance frameworks that address data privacy, IP and AI ethics ensures that the institution's AI systems are legally sound and ethically responsible. These frameworks should be reviewed and updated regularly to reflect changes in the legal landscape. Working closely with AI vendors helps ensure that third-party AI solutions are compliant with legal and ethical standards. Vendors should be required to demonstrate that their AI products adhere to current regulations and ethical guidelines, minimising the risk of non-compliance. Institutions must consider legal and regulatory compliance from the very beginning of AI tool development or acquisition. By designing AI systems with compliance in mind, institutions can avoid costly retroactive modifications that may be required to bring outdated systems in line with new regulations.

7.3.3 Maintaining a Dynamic AI Strategy

The fast-paced nature of AI technology necessitates a dynamic AI strategy that evolves alongside technological advancements, regulatory changes and educational needs. To stay ahead, institutions must review and update their AI strategy periodically to ensure alignment with both their institutional goals and the external environment. AI strategies should not be static documents. Institutions must conduct regular reviews to assess the effectiveness of their AI tools, identify areas for improvement and adjust to emerging trends. These reviews should consider factors such as new educational methodologies, changes in student needs and the availability of new AI technologies. AI strategies must align with the institution's broader mission and educational objectives. Whether the goal is to enhance student learning outcomes, improve operational efficiency or advance legal research, the AI strategy should clearly outline how AI tools contribute to these goals. This alignment ensures that AI investments provide measurable value to the institution.

7.3.4 Developing Technological Roadmaps

A forward-looking technological roadmap is crucial for guiding the long-term integration of AI into legal education. These roadmaps offer a strategic vision for how AI technologies will evolve and be implemented over time. By forecasting potential advancements in AI technology, institutions can plan for future upgrades and transitions. For example, as AI-driven legal research tools become more sophisticated, institutions should anticipate the need for integrating these tools into their curricula and research programmes. A technological roadmap helps ensure that AI investments are sustainable over the long term. It outlines key milestones for AI adoption, potential upgrades and necessary training programmes for faculty and staff. This forward-looking perspective prevents AI systems from becoming obsolete or misaligned with institutional needs as technology evolves.

7.3.5 Fostering a Culture of Innovation

To keep AI solutions relevant and on the cutting edge, institutions must cultivate a culture of innovation that encourages faculty, staff and students to propose new AI applications and improvements. Creating an environment that embraces technological experimentation and continuous improvement helps keep AI at the forefront of legal education. Faculty and staff are often the most familiar with the practical challenges of legal education and can offer valuable insights into how AI can address these challenges. Institutions should provide platforms for faculty and staff to suggest new AI applications, share best practices and collaborate on AI-related projects. Institutions can further foster innovation by supporting AI research and development efforts. By encouraging interdisciplinary collaborations among computer scientists, legal scholars and AI ethicists, institutions can drive innovation in AI applications tailored to legal education. Highlighting successful AI initiatives within the institution can inspire others to explore new AI possibilities. Organising showcases, seminars and workshops where faculty and students can present their AI-related projects helps create a culture of knowledge sharing and continuous improvement.

7.3.6 Balancing Innovation With Compliance

While innovation is essential for staying at the forefront of AI technology, it must be balanced with legal and ethical compliance. Institutions should ensure that new AI applications are vetted thoroughly by legal and compliance teams to confirm that they adhere to all relevant regulations. Institutions can maintain a balance between innovation and compliance by developing ethical frameworks that guide AI experimentation. By embedding compliance and ethical considerations into the institution's innovation process, legal education institutions can embrace AI advancements without compromising on legal and ethical standards.

Strategic updates are a cornerstone of successfully implementing and maintaining AI solutions in legal education. By staying ahead of regulatory changes, establishing legal and compliance teams and maintaining a dynamic AI strategy, institutions can ensure that their AI systems are both innovative and compliant. Developing technological roadmaps and fostering a culture of innovation further ensures that AI remains a central, evolving part of legal education. By proactively balancing innovation with compliance, legal education institutions can create a robust AI ecosystem that enhances learning, operational efficiency and research while adhering to the highest legal and ethical standards.

Practical Tips

By adopting these strategies and principles, legal education institutions can address the long-term viability of AI solutions proactively. This approach ensures that AI continues to deliver value, remains aligned with sustainability goals and effectively serves the evolving educational needs of the institution and its stakeholders over time. Several challenges are associated with ensuring the long-term viability of AI solutions in legal education, as outlined in the following. These challenges include technical, financial, regulatory and institutional aspects, each requiring careful consideration and proactive management.

Rapid Technological Obsolescence

AI technology evolves at a rapid pace, meaning that solutions that are on the cutting edge today may become obsolete within a few years. Legal education institutions may struggle to keep up with these changes due to the high costs of upgrading AI infrastructure and the need for constant training of staff and faculty. This creates pressure on institutions to continuously invest in new technologies, potentially straining budgets and creating disruptions in educational practices. Institutions need to adopt scalable, adaptable AI systems that can evolve with technological advancements, but this requires significant upfront planning and resources.

Evolving Educational Needs

As legal education shifts towards new pedagogical models such as experiential learning or competency-based education, AI tools must adapt to these changes. However, aligning AI solutions with evolving educational trends can be challenging and requires ongoing collaboration between educators and technologists. If AI tools are not flexible enough to accommodate these shifts, they may become irrelevant or ineffective, resulting in wasted investments and diminished educational outcomes. Developing AI systems that are versatile and continuously aligned with educational goals requires a commitment to regular reassessment and updating of AI strategies.

High Initial and Ongoing Costs

AI solutions require significant upfront investments in hardware, software and training. Additionally, there are ongoing costs for system updates, maintenance and cybersecurity measures. For many institutions, especially those with limited resources, these costs can be prohibitive. The high cost of implementing and maintaining AI solutions may deter some institutions from adopting AI or lead to insufficient investment in crucial areas such as cybersecurity and staff training, which could undermine long-term viability. Conducting comprehensive cost–benefit analyses and ROI assessments can help institutions plan more effectively, but balancing costs with educational outcomes remains difficult.

Scalability and Adaptability Issues

Ensuring that AI systems can scale with changes in student enrolment, curriculum shifts and emerging technological trends is essential, but many AI solutions may lack the flexibility needed for long-term scalability. Systems that cannot scale easily may become bottlenecks as demand for AI-driven education grows, or they may not meet the changing needs of the institution. Institutions need to carefully evaluate AI vendors and solutions for scalability, but this requires technical expertise and long-term strategic planning, which can be difficult to maintain.

Regulatory and Legal Compliance

Legal education institutions must comply with a growing number of regulations related to data privacy, IP and the ethical use of AI. These regulations are constantly evolving, which makes maintaining compliance difficult and resource intensive. Failure to comply with new regulations could result in legal penalties, ethical violations and reputational damage, especially since legal education deals with sensitive data such as client information and case studies. Institutions must invest in legal expertise and compliance monitoring, but staying up to date with regulatory changes is a continuous burden.

User Experience and Engagement

AI-driven tools need to be user-friendly and well integrated into educational practices to ensure widespread adoption by students and educators. However, poor user experiences can result in low engagement, rendering AI solutions ineffective despite significant investment. If users do not engage with AI tools, institutions may not see the expected educational benefits, leading to a waste of resources and decreased enthusiasm for future AI implementation. Ensuring positive user experiences requires ongoing feedback mechanisms and updates, but designing intuitive systems that meet the diverse needs of students and faculty can be complex.

Institutional Resistance to Change

Faculty and administrators may resist the integration of AI into legal education due to unfamiliarity with the technology, concerns about job security or scepticism about the benefits of AI. This resistance can slow down AI adoption and limit its potential impact. Resistance to change can hinder the institution's ability to adapt to technological advancements, leaving it behind competitors that more fully embrace AI. Cultivating a culture of innovation and providing training and support for faculty and staff can help overcome this challenge, but institutional change is often slow and difficult to achieve.

Sustainability of AI Infrastructure

Maintaining the infrastructure that supports AI systems – such as data centres, servers and cloud services – requires significant energy consumption, contributing to environmental concerns. Additionally, the rapid turnover of hardware due to obsolescence contributes to e-waste. These environmental impacts can undermine the institution's sustainability goals and lead to increased operational costs in the long term. Institutions need to adopt energy-efficient technologies and develop e-waste management strategies, but this adds additional layers of complexity and cost to AI implementation.

Balancing Innovation With Ethical Considerations

Legal education institutions must balance the need for AI innovation with ethical considerations, including data privacy, bias in AI algorithms and the potential for AI to replace human educators in certain contexts. Addressing these concerns while still advancing technological solutions can be difficult. Ethical missteps could result in public backlash, legal challenges or harm to students and educators, ultimately limiting the potential of AI in legal education. Developing comprehensive ethical frameworks and promoting transparency in AI use can help, but enforcing these principles consistently across an institution requires considerable effort.

The long-term viability of AI solutions in legal education is shaped by a combination of technical, financial, regulatory and institutional challenges. Institutions must be proactive in addressing these challenges through strategic planning, continuous evaluation and adaptability. While AI presents tremendous opportunities for improving legal education, ensuring its sustainability requires ongoing commitment and a willingness to evolve with the changing landscape. By adopting these strategies, legal education institutions can ensure the long-term viability of AI solutions. Proactive planning, regular evaluation and adaptability will ensure that AI technologies continue to deliver value, remain aligned with the institution's sustainability goals and address the evolving needs of students, faculty and legal professionals. In doing so, institutions can maintain a forward-thinking approach to AI in legal education, ensuring that AI-driven solutions remain a sustainable and integral part of their educational landscape.

Conclusion

The integration of AI into legal education represents a profound shift with far-reaching implications. While AI holds immense promise in enhancing efficiency, accessibility and innovation in legal education, it also presents significant ethical and sustainability challenges. Addressing the environmental, ethical and societal dimensions of AI adoption in legal education is, however, imperative for ensuring a responsible and sustainable future for the legal profession. This book has examined the intricate intersection of AI adoption, sustainability ethics and legal education, emphasising the imperative for a conscientious application of sustainability principles. The ethical dimensions of AI adoption in legal education are many, encompassing issues such as algorithmic bias, data privacy and equitable access to AI-driven resources. Addressing these challenges requires a comprehensive framework for promoting fairness, inclusivity and ethical AI initiatives. Ethical considerations loom large in the AI-powered legal landscape. Striking a balance between AI's potential benefits and its potential biases and inequities is a critical sustainability challenge. Legal education must equip future lawyers with the knowledge and ethical frameworks to navigate these complexities responsibly. Additionally, sustainability considerations extend beyond environmental concerns to encompass social justice, equity and the long-term viability of educational practices. The integration of AI into legal education, while promising transformative benefits, is therefore not without significant sustainability challenges.

Strategies for promoting sustainable AI adoption in legal education include integrating AI law, ethics and sustainability into the curriculum, developing resource allocation strategies and implementing faculty training programmes. Moreover, collaboration, strategic leadership and a focus on critical thinking skills are all essential for responsibly navigating the complex landscape of AI integration. As legal education institutions strive to embrace AI in a sustainable and ethical manner, they must consider various push and pull factors, including budgetary constraints, infrastructure limitations and the expectations of external stakeholders. By advocating for sustainable solutions and fostering collaboration among stakeholders, legal education can lead the way

DOI: 10.4324/9781003607397-9

in shaping a future where AI serves as a valuable tool while upholding ethical standards and environmental stewardship. Furthermore, the societal responsibility of legal education extends to addressing the digital divide, ensuring that all students have equitable access to AI-driven resources and knowledge. Sustainable strategies to bridge this divide are essential for fostering inclusivity. As we prepare legal professionals for the future, we must recognise that sustainability is not just an environmental concern but also a holistic concept that encompasses social, ethical and long-term viability dimensions. The journey towards sustainable AI adoption in legal education requires collaboration, innovation and a commitment to ethical practice.

In essence, sustainable AI adoption in legal education necessitates a holistic and forward-thinking approach that carefully balances the potential benefits of AI with critical ethical considerations and sustainability imperatives. Legal education is at a crossroads where emerging AI technologies can provide transformative opportunities in terms of efficiency, accessibility and innovation. However, these advancements must not come at the expense of ethical integrity, social justice and environmental responsibility. By taking a comprehensive approach that integrates sustainability into every aspect of AI adoption – from curriculum development and faculty training to infrastructure and policy design – institutions can ensure that AI becomes an enabler of positive change rather than a source of unintended harm. Addressing these challenges requires proactive measures that focus on both the immediate and long-term implications of AI use in legal education. First, institutions must ensure that AI systems are designed and implemented with ethical frameworks in mind, taking into account issues such as algorithmic bias, data privacy and equitable access. Legal education, which trains future lawyers and policymakers, has a unique responsibility to model ethical practices in its own adoption of AI technologies. Institutions must establish governance structures that provide oversight and accountability, ensuring that AI is used responsibly and in line with the core values of the legal profession.

In addition to ethics, sustainability is paramount in the context of AI adoption. Sustainable AI in legal education means not only reducing the environmental impact of AI systems through energy-efficient technologies and responsible data management practices, but also addressing the social dimensions of sustainability. This includes bridging the digital divide by ensuring that students from all backgrounds have equal access to AI-driven tools and resources. Inclusivity is central to creating a more equitable and just educational environment, where the benefits of AI are shared across the student body and not limited to those with greater financial resources or technological access. By addressing these challenges head-on, institutions can harness the transformative power of AI while simultaneously safeguarding the ethical and sustainable practices that underpin the legal profession. AI has the potential to revolutionise legal education, providing new ways to engage students, improve learning outcomes and streamline administrative processes.

However, this transformation must be guided by a commitment to sustainability, ensuring that AI is not only efficient and innovative but also aligned with the long-term well-being of society and the planet. Moreover, sustainability in AI adoption extends to the lifespan of AI technologies themselves. AI tools and systems evolve rapidly, and institutions must remain adaptable to changing technological landscapes. This means investing in scalable, flexible and future-proof AI solutions that can grow and adapt alongside advancements in both legal education and AI technology. Regular evaluations of AI initiatives, including cost–benefit analyses and assessments of their impact on students and faculty, are essential for ensuring that AI systems remain relevant, ethical and sustainable over time.

Ultimately, it is through these efforts of conscious and responsible AI adoption that we can shape a future where AI serves as a valuable tool in legal education while preserving the well-being of our environment, society and ethical standards. Legal education institutions have a unique opportunity to lead by example, demonstrating how AI can be used to advance both educational goals and broader societal values. By embracing a holistic approach to AI adoption that balances technological innovation with ethical responsibility and sustainability, we can ensure that AI contributes to the betterment of both the legal profession and the world at large. This forward-thinking mindset will not only prepare future lawyers to navigate the complexities of an AI-driven legal landscape but also instil in them the values of responsibility, justice and sustainability that will guide their careers and influence the development of AI policies and practices in the years to come.